# DEAD

# CERTAINTIES

(UNWARRANTED SPECULATIONS)

# DEAD

# CERTAINTIES

## (UNWARRANTED SPECULATIONS)

# Simon Schama

ALFRED A. KNOPF  NEW YORK 1991

A portion of this work was originally published
in *Granta* magazine.

Grateful acknowledgement is made to
Farrar, Straus & Giroux, Inc., for permission to reprint
from "History" from *Selected Poems* by Robert Lowell.
Copyright © 1973, 1976 by Robert Lowell.

Library of Congress Cataloging-in-Publication Data
Schama, Simon.
Dead certainties : unwarranted speculations /
Simon Schama. — 1st ed.
p.      cm.
ISBN 0-679-40213-6
1. Boston (Mass.)—Biography. 2. Wolfe, James,
1727–1759—Death and burial. 3. Parkman, Francis,
1823–1893—Death and burial. 4. Parkman, George,
1790–1849—Death and burial. 5. Death—Social
aspects—Massachusetts—Boston—History. I. Title.
F73.25.S33     1991
974.4'6103'0922—dc20
[B]          90-52902     CIP

Manufactured in the United States of America
First Edition

In memory of John Clive,
for whom history was literature

History has to live with what was here,
clutching and close to fumbling all we had—
it is so dull and gruesome how we die,
unlike writing, life never finishes.

— ROBERT LOWELL, "History"

# Contents

# Acknowledgements

I should like to thank the archivists and librarians of the Massachusetts Historical Society without whose kindness and zeal I could never have made my way through the documentary labyrinth of the Webster case. I am also grateful to the Society for permission to quote extensively from their archives. The staff of the Harvard University Archive were also extremely helpful, especially in tracking down Edward Sohier's obituary.

Even though my wife, Ginny Papaioannou, has had to listen to endless recitals on the theme of the Parkmans, Brahmin Boston, and John White Webster, she gave the manuscript her usual vigilant reading, offered many important suggestions and corrections and above all sustained my occasionally wavering faith in the enterprise with loving good sense.

Bill Buford and Bob Tashman of *Granta* first encouraged me to pursue the experiment with historical narrative that became *The Many Deaths of General Wolfe,* and then to follow my curiosity about the death of George Parkman into the archive and out again onto the pages of their extraordinary magazine. It has been a delight to work with them. As always my many friends at Alfred A. Knopf—Carol Janeway, Robin Swados, Nancy Clements and Iris Weinstein—have had the collective genius of turning notions into a book. And to my two pillars of strength, Peter Matson and Michael Sissons, who have had to calm me down, cheer me up, cheer me on and occasionally pick up the pieces, I am, as always, more grateful than I can ever really let them know.

*One*

# The Many Deaths of
# General Wolfe

George Townshend, *Portrait of James Wolfe* (1759)

# 1
# At the Face of the Cliff

*Anse du Foulon, Quebec, four a.m., September 13, 1759*

'Twas the darkness that did the trick, black as tar, that and the silence, though how the men contriv'd to clamber their way up the cliff with their musket and seventy rounds on their backs, I'm sure I don't know even though I saw it with my own eyes and did it myself before very long. We stood hushed on the muddy shore of the river, peering up at the volunteers. They looked like a pack of lizards unloosd on the rocks, though not so nimble, bellies hugging the cliff and their rumps wiggling with the effort. We couldn't see much of 'em for they disappeared now and then into the clumps of witherd cedar and spruce that hung on the side of the hill. But we could feel the squirming, pulling labour of it all. And by God they were quiet alright. Now and then a man's boot would find a foothold he thought secure and away would come a shower of soft dirt, near taking the fellow with him down the cliff. Curses come to a soldier as easy as breathing, but we heard none that night, not at the start of it all. Some scoundrel later put it about that the General himself had struck off the head of a man who curs'd too loud when he dropped his pack to still any who should think to do the same. But that was never the General's way. Though he had the temper in him of a red-hair'd man, he was an orderly commander who lik'd things done by the Regulations and it would go damnd hard on any poor infantryman who thought to help himself to the spoils of war, be it just a goat or a pig, when all the killing and running were done.

I suppose the silence told Wolfe the game was in earnest. For had bodies come tumbling down or firing started from the top he would have stopped it right there and then. For all his soldierly zeal he was rattled by the cliff when he had jumpd from the landing boat and come to its face, and could see the height of it, near enough two hundred feet and the sheerness of it. "I dont think we can by any possible means get up here," we heard him say, "but we must use our best endeavour." And so it fell to the turn of the Twenty-Eighth and we started to haul ourselves over the black limestone, reaching for stumps and scrubby patches of choke-cherries and hawthorn that covered the nether part of the hill. By such cumbersome means we lugged ourselves up a bit at a time, skinning our hands, dirtying our breeches and praying the next bit of scrawny stick and leaf was deep enough rooted to hold us up. One thing was sure, our coats and leggings weren't made for such work, for they flapped and pinchd as we dragged ourselves up; and I could swear the Rangers who were fitter dress'd for it sniggerd as they saw us struggling with our tackle. Indeed the whole business seemd perilous, vertical folly and nothing the King of Prussia would have commended. We all feard it might yet go badly as it had done in July at the Montmorency Falls where the French had peppered us with grapeshot and the drenching rain had turned the hill into a filthy slide. Men had come tumbling down in a mess of blood and mud and fear, and those that couldn't run were left to face the Savages as best they could, poor beggars.

But our fortunes were fairer that night for when the sentries challengd our boats as we saild upriver, Mr. Fraser he answered them in French good enough to pass and even threw in an oath or two against the English *bougres* for good measure. And we were all glad of the Scotchmen this time, even the Highlanders, for of Delaune's first men up the rocks they were all Macphersons and Macdougals and Camerons and the like. A good crew for a general who had fought on Culloden Field! And here too they did the King good service for I had no sooner got to the very top and was rejoicing and taking good care not to look down behind

me when our men gathered together amidst the
tamaracks and the spruce. Before us were a group
of tents, white in the first thin light of the coming
dawn, and of a sudden a commotion and shouting
broke forth. A Frenchy officer came flying out in
his nightshirt as we loosd off our first rounds and
sent them running across the open fields towards
the town leaving a few of their company shot or
stuck with our bayonets wearing that surprisd look
on their face as they lay there amidst the pine
needles and brown grass.

Once the peace was broken and we were masters of the place and the French guns, we set up a
huzzaing and men down below threw themselves
at the hill, Wolfe first of all, they said, and suddenly
the rocks were alive with soldiers, Rangers and
Highlanders and Grenadiers groping their way to
the top. Monckton even managed to find a zig-zag
path, two men wide, to lug our field-pieces up. The
boats that had dischargd the first men went back to
fetch some more from the ships, and after an hour
or two we stood in the dawn light, a cool spraying
rain coming down, maybe four thousand of us,
more than we had dar'd hope but not so many I still
thought as would come to a prize fight at Bar-
tholomews Fair, too few for the business.

Monckton and Barré formd us up again in our
lines, smartly enough. The Grenadiers formed to
our right and the Forty-Third, Forty-Seventh and

the Highlanders to our left, Mr. Burton's Forty-Eighth behind us in reserve and Townshend and the Fifteenth at right angles. Better though our situation was than we might have expected, there was not a man jack of us but didnt feel the scare of the battle crawling through his uniform and was glad of the two days rum we had got issued. The General put some heart in us, coming to our lines to talk of duty and the King and what our country expected of us and all of Canada at our mercy if we but prevaild this once. After he died they made him look like a Roman, even on the penny prints I have seen, but he lookd no Roman to us. For though he was six foot, he carried that height queerly, in a loping gait, with his bony frame and sloping shoulders ending in a poke-up neck. What was on top of it bore little resemblance to the Antiques either, what with his pop eyes and his little chins wobbling under his jaw, his skin the colour of cheese and a snout on him like a ferret. Nor was he much a humorous man, more in the melancholy way. Brigadier Townshend did some scribbles of him peering at the latrines or measuring the height of his reputation which got passed around the camp and gave us some mirth in the midst of all our adversities, but they pleasd their subject not at all. Yet he was a good general to trust, even if it was his fancy to call us "brother soldiers," for he was fearless and would walk before the men under fire, pointing his cane like Old Gideon's staff, and we followed sure enough.

## The Life of General Wolfe

By seven o'clock the low clouds and drizzle that hung over the Heights of Abraham had given way to a gentle sunshine. Wolfe and his three brigadiers—Murray, the dependable Monckton and the erratic Townshend—had placed their lines in battle order. For the first time in the whole campaign, it was the British who waited, the French who had to react. A stillness descended on the grassy plain, broken only by the occasional crack of musket fire coming from Indian and Canadian shooters hidden in the woods to the left of the British lines.

For James Wolfe it had come to this, at last. Months of misery and frustration, of failing to winkle out Montcalm's troops from their citadel of Quebec, much less dislodging the batteries on the north shore of the St. Lawrence, had finally found some resolution. The humiliation of his position had galled him, and he was not eased by the embarrassing recollection of drunken, swaggering boasts made to William Pitt on the eve of his departure. Once up the river he had realized how daunting his mission was; how idle the hope of dividing Montcalm's army or provoking it to come down from its fortified heights and engage. Nor had his proclamation, written, he thought, in the most sententious French at his command, been effective even though it had exuded magnanimity and had spoken honourably of the protection of the Canadians' religion and their property, and given an assurance that he had come not "to destroy and depopulate" but merely to "subdue" and "bring them into subjection to the King his master." In vexation he had begun to bombard Quebec from the positions set up by the fleet, so that a steady deafening rain of mortars and shells fell on the town, day and night.

But what good had this done except to assuage the endless sense of impotence and rage that swelled inside him as spring turned into a scorching, dripping, foul-smelling summer? His troops were falling sick from putrid fevers and were tormented by blackfly that with their stinging bites could cover a man's face or arms with gobs of blood. When it became apparent that so far from joining themselves to the protection of His Majesty the Canadian trappers and farmers had sent their women and children to the town, while the men had formed irregular companies to harass the troops, a second proclamation, angrier than the first, announced the coming of "violent" measures both to punish and deter. Farm cabins and whole villages had been destroyed, corn burned in the fields. But in return they had the Indians—Abenakis and Iroquois—to contend with, lying in wait for their raiding parties. And of what the Savages were said and known to do, their scalping and tomahawking, the troops were in shuddering terror. Men returned to camp unmanned, with stories of slivers of wood pushed up the penis and behind their nails and more than ever they came to feel they were being sacrificed to some vanity of the General and his thirst for reputation.

So the landing at the Montmorency Falls had been determined as much by the need to do *something* to force the issue, as by any calculated hope of success. Wolfe was agonized by the possibility of returning to England not in a chorus of Handelian Hosannas but in a cloud of ignominy. How would he dare face Amherst, the commander of the expedition, or Pitt, who had been so criticized for putting his faith in a stripling major-general still in his thirties? He dreaded the jeering of the merciless coffee-house press; the caricaturists for whom his peculiar physiognomy must have seemed heaven-sent; the howling catcalls of the theatre as some half-drunk actor bawled a profane air at his expense. How could he greet his betrothed, who overlooked his curious phiz and figure and his graceless manner as the eccentricities of one born for a heroic fate? How could he look his father, the General, in the eye, and worst of all what would he say to his exacting, adamant mother?

## At the Face of the Cliff

But the landing had been horribly botched. The French had prudently refused to descend to engage the British force and had been content to inflict a murderous fire from their batteries on the haplessly climbing soldiers, defenceless and falling over each other in rain-sodden confusion. Painfully aware that he was losing the authority of his command, each day watching his force being eaten up by sickness, boredom and desertion, Wolfe increasingly kept his own counsel and brooded sourly on the disappointment of his hopes. The chivalrous major-general who had exchanged cases of wine with his adversary, the Marquis de Montcalm, who had promised peace and conciliation, now displayed fits of vindictive petulance. Orders were given sending raids deeper into the country to exterminate Canadian settlements at the same time as British guns were obliterating the timbered houses of Old Quebec itself.

Wolfe was running two races, and in both, time seemed to be against him. Unless he found some way to pry the French army from its lair, the swift icing of the St. Lawrence would close his fleet in and cut its supply line from the Louisbourg peninsula at the river's mouth. But there was a greater enemy than the river and the season; greater yet than the damnably canny Montcalm, and that was his own body. He had always been preoccupied by his physical frailty and had even been capable of dark banter on the subject. "If I Say I am thinner," he had written to his friend Rickson, "you will imagine me a shadow or a skeleton in motion. In short I am everything but what the surgeons call a subject for anatomy. As far as muscles, bones and the larger vessels conserve their purpose they have a clear view of them in me, distinct from fat or fleshy impediment. . . ."

But now, he thought, he was dying, withering away of gravel and consumption; a raging, scalding venom that ate at his guts. His bladder was a failing vessel; his kidneys, demons that racked him day and night. It was torture to piss and worse not to piss and periodically he suffered the indignities of dysentery, too. Somehow, though, he grimly preserved his composure, for the sake of his men and for the duty he had taken on. The surgeon bled him profusely, and together with his want of sleep, there arose in his naturally wan features a ghostly mouldy pallor from which big eyes glittered in their darkened sockets.

An escape from this death by degrees — of both the expedition itself and its commander — finally presented itself (as escapes so often do) by way of a response to a secondary problem. Thinking of how to intercept Quebec's supply lines from Montreal to the west, Wolfe's officers and Admiral Saunders, the commander of the fleet, conceived the plan of sailing up-river, past Quebec itself, to a point where a force might interpose itself between the city and its rear. Wolfe himself needed persuading, all the more so since he increasingly mistrusted one of his three brigadiers, the overtly disaffected George Townshend whose natural irreverence and sardonic manner were, Wolfe thought, coming damnably close to insubordination. Once convinced of the idea of an attack from behind, Wolfe converted it from a tactical element in the campaign to the strategy on which victory or defeat would necessarily turn. The risks were alarming since the known landing-sites were heavily fortified with batteries, and wherever the guns were less in evidence, the escarpment seemed too sheer to allow any kind of ascent. The only chance of success lay with careful subterfuge and surprise. A flotilla was to go up-river with the flood tide, beyond its apparent landing, and then allow the ebb, calculated for four in the morning, to drift landing-craft back to the shore. But such was Wolfe's mounting mistrust and anxiety that he refused to divulge to his own senior officers the exact location of this landing, forcing them to write to him for an answer so the plan would not be put in jeopardy.

Wolfe was painfully conscious that the moment that beckoned him was one to which his whole life had been pointing. Since he was a child he had known nothing, nor expected anything, other than the army career in which his father had achieved some rank and modest renown. James had left for camp when he was fourteen, had been an adjutant at Dettingen at sixteen where two horses had been shot from under him and at nineteen had eagerly joined the slaughter of Jacobites at Culloden and Falkirk. Yet nothing much had come of these youthful exertions. He had ended up quartered in Ireland, grumbling in a prematurely bilious way about the corruption, debauchery and insolence of the natives. The coming of another war with France in 1756 seemed to offer liberation from boredom and hypochondria, but instead it enfolded him in fiasco. The amphibious expedition to the Atlantic port of Rochefort had ended up bobbing indeterminately in the roadstead while the naval commander bickered with the army commander about what to do and when to do it. Wolfe was one of the few officers exonerated in the subsequent investigation and was promoted to brigadier for the siege of Louisbourg at the mouth of the St. Lawrence, French Canada's lifeline to its homeland. While that stronghold eventually fell in 1758, Wolfe regarded the siege as wasteful, prolonged and incompetent and lost no opportunity in letting this be known when he returned on leave at the end of that year.

His reputation had remained unsullied, indeed had even blossomed, as the British imperial war effort staggered from mishap to mishap. When William Pitt, the gouty, bloody-minded genius of global strategy, designed one for America of crushing simplicity, Wolfe was given a commission of crucial significance. There would be a two-pronged onslaught on French America that would be decisive: one to the fort of Ticonderoga in the Appalachians, and an amphibious expedition up the St. Lawrence to Quebec and Montreal. If successful, the two attacks would join at the upper Ohio and sever the line of containment France had constructed from Canada to the Mississippi basin against the westward expansion of the British colonies.

Wolfe had always hungered for such a responsibility, but now that it had come, it seemed more a burden than an opportunity. Perhaps Pitt had recognised in him a fellow neurotic, driven by the volatile mixture of monomania, dejection and elation that fired all the most formidable military imperialists. Exactly to type, Wolfe alternated between undignified self-congratulation and self-reproach. He was, he thought, riddled with shortcomings that would be his undoing. His physique deteriorated sympathetically with this onset of mercurial energy and sent him to Bath to take the waters. It was there that he met Katherine Lowther, handsome, articulate and rich, the daughter of the Governor of Barbados (where one became very rich indeed), who was abominated almost everywhere else.

·    ·    ·

Wolfe had been in love once before, at twenty-one when he had paid court to Elizabeth Lawson (as plain as Katherine Lowther was good-looking). Though "sweet-tempered," she was seriously disabled in the eyes of General and Mrs. Wolfe by her modest fortune. They had made their own selection for their son, which he in turn rejected. Parents and son then compromised by forgetting about marriage altogether. Once hot with passion, Wolfe cooled rapidly as he distanced himself from his love and got on with war and advancement. He was ten years older when he met Katherine; she commanded a rank and fortune that Wolfe must have presumed would sweep aside any parental reservations. He was sadly disabused of this unwarranted optimism. Henrietta Wolfe remained implacable in her displeasure, unmoveable in her objections. A frosty hostility descended on a relationship which until recently had been suffocatingly close. Wolfe visited the family house at Blackheath just once during his three-month winter leave and instead of bidding his parents farewell sent a letter of bleak severity to his mother:

DEAR MADAM,—The formality of taking leave should be as much as possible avoided; therefore I prefer this method of offering my good wishes and duty to my father and you. I shall carry this business through with the best of my abilities. The rest you know, is in the hands of Providence, to whose care I hope your good life and conduct will recommend your son. . . . I heartily wish you health and enjoyment of the many good things that have fallen to your share. My best duty to the General.

I am, dear Madam,

Your obedient and affectionate son,

JAM; WOLFE

He took with him on *The Neptune* a miniature portrait of Katherine, whom in his correspondence he greets as his lover and implies a betrothal that was none the less left unannounced and unofficial. To his Uncle Walter in Dublin (yet another military Wolfe) he confided his plan both to marry Katherine and to leave the service if the weakness of his constitution allowed him to see his commission through to a victorious conclusion. He also had with him Katherine's copy of Gray's "Elegy in a Country Churchyard," which he annotated heavily during the long, miserable, nauseating voyage. It was this poem, lugubriously beautiful in its meter and metaphor, and universally admired by Wolfe's generation, that gave rise to the most famous piece of Wolfiana: that on the eve of battle the General recited it to his soldiers. If in fact he did (and the sources are strong enough to resist the automatic modern assumption of apocrypha), it could hardly have raised their spirits even if it moved their souls, concluding as it did with the prophecy that *the paths of glory lead but to the grave.*" "I can only say, Gentlemen," he is reported to have declared at its end, "that if the choice were mine I would rather be the author of those verses than win the battle which we are to fight to-morrow morning."

But Wolfe was always more than a waver of flags and a rattler of sabres. His driven, febrile person-ality, swinging between tender compassion and angry vanity, was haunted by Night Thoughts, by ravens perched on tombstones. If he was an empire-builder he knew he was also a grave-digger, perhaps his own. When he was feeling most embattled on the St. Lawrence, the news came to him of his father's death. This was not a shock since, as he had written to Uncle Walter, "I left him in so weak a condition that it was not probable we should meet again." But Wolfe's foreknowledge makes the chilling circumstances of his departure from England even more depress-ing. The "general tenor" of his father's life, he wrote, "has been extremely upright [so that] be-nevolent and little feelings of imperfections were overbalanced by his many good qualities." Having delivered himself of this overly judicious obituary, Wolfe betrayed a pathetic solitude; he was increas-ingly convinced that, whether by fire or fever, he would not survive to become a husband. "I know you cannot cure my complaint," he told his sur-geon, "but patch me up so I may be able to do my

enjamin West, *The Death of General Wolfe* (1770)

duty for the next few days and I shall be content."
His will, dictated to his aides-de-camp shortly before the decisive battle, asked for Katherine's portrait to be set with five hundred guineas' worth of
jewels and then returned to her.

To the elegiac resignation of Gray, Wolfe may
have added his own Augustan conception of the
Hero. For he also transcribed lines from Pope's
translation of the *Iliad* together with his own inel-
egant but telling alterations:

> *But since, alas! ignoble age must come*
> *Disease and death's inexorable doom,*
> *The life which others pay, let us bestow,*
> *And give to Fame what we to Nature owe*
> *Brave let us fall or honoured if we live*
> *Or let us glory gain or glory give . . .*

The night came; the flotilla set off. Challenged
with a *"Qui vive?"* the French-speaking Scot
obliged with *"La France,"* and persuaded the
guards stationed above the river that they were a
provisions fleet. *"Laissez les passer,"* came the reassuring response. A gentle September breeze got
up, rippling the water as the boats drifted along the
high banks lined with walls of fir trees pointing at
the stars. In the early hours, at their station, men
were dropped into the landing boats which drifted
back on the ebb; Wolfe sat bolt upright in one of

them, anxious lest they overshoot their mark, which they duly did. So be it. It had to be this or nothing. He held in his hands the design of his posterity. By making Britain's history he could at last make his own. He was at the cliff face.

# 2
# In Command

*The Royal Academy Exhibition Gallery, Pall Mall,*
*April 29, 1771*

It was the light that did the trick; a clean, shrewdly directed radiance illuminating the face of the martyr and bathing the grieving expressions of his brother officers in a reflection of impossible holiness. Benjamin West picked up this piece of artfulness from the stage (along with his device of arranging spectators on a platform projecting through the picture space as though it were a proscenium). In the theatre, candle-footlights or a hooped chandelier would highlight action on centre stage against a background of carefully darkened obscurity from which characters would emerge or dissolve. West went one better by tearing back a patch of black cloud to expose a space of cerulean, celestial blue sky through which the sun shone; a light of sacred purity that seemed to embrace the expiring Hero. It was a stupendous piece of drama: brilliance and gloom, victory and death, saintly sacrifice and inconsolable sorrow set side by side, the sunlit sky of the imperial future banishing the grim clouds of past dissatisfactions. The public adored grandstanding performances and responded to this one with rapture. Asked by a spectator whether the painter had correctly caught the expression of a dying man, David Garrick was said to have thrown himself on the floor in the appropriate posture. The gallery rang with applause.

On April 29, 1771, the *Gentleman's Magazine* reported that an earthquake had struck Abingdon, Berkshire. Though of but a moment's duration, it had lifted men and women off the ground while they were in their chairs. Others had felt the pavement sway and pitch. Something of the same sense of elation and terror, shock and anguish was experienced by the crowds at Pall Mall on the morning when West's painting, famous in rumour even before its exhibition, was at last exhibited. Lines had formed down the street for admission to the Royal Academy's galleries. A great deal of porter got drunk, a great many of Tiddy Dol's pies gnawed on to appease the growing impatience. Only the spectacle of so many high personages entering before the others offered some diversion. The crowd saw come and go: Lord Temple, William Pitt (now Lord Chatham), ancient and tottering on his bandaged legs and crutches. He was later said to have spent much time before the painting, but to have complained about the general dejection to which the principals seemed (not surprisingly) to have succumbed. The famous and notorious beauty Georgiana, the Duchess of Devonshire, who had sketched Wolfe herself, came and went as conspicuously as possible; Horace Walpole offered predictably faint praise. The unimaginably wealthy Lord Richard Grosvenor attended; he had bought the painting for the outrageous sum of four hundred guineas, and many thought it had been commissioned for him in the first place. Finally the King arrived, and he had let it be known in advance that he did not want it.

George III, unlike his father, alongside whom Wolfe had fought at Dettingen, displayed a taste in painting that belied his reputation for bucolic simplicity. He was in fact the most sophisticated royal collector since Charles I (whom he much admired in other, not altogether agreeable, respects). His patronage, bestowed on the young and relatively obscure American artist five years earlier, had abruptly propelled West to celebrity and fortune. The King had heard something from his agents in Rome of a Pennsylvanian prodigy who was studying there at the time of his accession, assiduously copying Antique sculpture and the Renaissance masters. But it had been West's first serious sponsor and patron, William Drummond, the Archbishop of York, who had brought him directly to the King's attention. The cleric had shown the King West's *Agrippina with the Ashes of Ger-*

*manicus at Brundisium,* in which a heroic procession files before the viewer on a shallow stage.
In the background the action dimly unfolds while
in the near foreground spectators turn towards the
principals in rapt attention. It was the kind of thing
the King liked: a history play in dignified motion,
full of uplifting emotions and virtuous allusions
but free of gimcrack mummery or Popish ob-
scurantism. It was, in short, that thing for which
the polite nation had been yearning: a British history painting.

On the strength of the *Agrippina,* West was
commissioned to do a second history, similar in
format and expressly for George III. The subject
was to be the Roman general Regulus departing
from his native city to return to Carthage. He had
been captured in the Punic Wars and allowed to
return home to help sue for peace. Once he was
there, however, his patriotic obligation required
him to speak the truth and counsel against such
an ignominious settlement of wrongs. Despite
the certain knowledge that he would be put to
death for his failure, his sense of honour obliged
him to return to his captors. By repeating all the
ingredients of the *Agrippina,* West guaranteed
that the King would be delighted, and so he was.
When he learned, however, that his favourite
painter was now contemplating a *Death of General
Wolfe* in which the figures were to be costumed in
modern dress rather than the togas or chitons of

the ancients, he let his dismay and displeasure be known.

There was another critic, whose authority had the power to do almost as much damage as the King's to West's career. In the same year that the American was working on the project that would surely make or break his reputation, Joshua Reynolds became *Sir* Joshua Reynolds. The honour was in recognition of his appointment as first President of the Royal Academy, itself only established in 1768. Reynolds was at the height of his powers, both as a virtuoso painter of portraits and histories and as a theorist who in his work had redefined the canons of classicism. His *Discourses,* first set out as annual addresses to the Fellows and students of the Academy, aimed to establish universal criteria for the conjunction of Truth and Beauty, embodied first in antiquity and set, eternally, as the goals to which all high and polite art must unswervingly aim.

Though they were perhaps a little enamoured of visual anecdote and a little more theatrical than Reynolds would have liked, there was nothing hitherto in West's histories to occasion serious objection. On the strength of the works exhibited at Spring Gardens and, more important, of the King's favour, the American had in fact become an Academician. But reports of West's intentions to present Wolfe's death in contemporary dress struck Reynolds as an act of appalling vulgarity.

John Galt, who in the 1820s wrote the first biography of West, made the story of Reynolds's and
West's encounter famous. No doubt (since Galt
wrote in accordance with West's elaborate wishes)
it gives a more heroic account of the artist's uncom-
promising determination than may have actually
been the case. Although self-serving and embel-
lished, it nonetheless gets the argument about
making histories exactly right.

Reynolds's objection was not simply the stuffy
complaint that West was violating convention. It
was rather that by reporting naturalistically on a
modern event he was robbing a history of the
universal significance which its narrative ought to
embody. If the history were to persuade and endure, it was imperative to find an idealised, universal language in which its exalted conceptions could
be represented, and not to distract the beholder
with a flashy and elaborate spectacle, heavy with
"minute particularities of dress." West's response,
as reported by Galt, was famously and invincibly
American.

I began by remarking that the event intended to be
commemorated took place on the 13th of September
1758 [a year off!] in a region of the world unknown to
the Greeks and Romans and at a period of time when
no such nation and heroes in their costume any longer
existed. The subject I have to represent is the conquest of a great province of America by the British
troops. It is a topic that history will proudly record and

the same truth that guides the pen of the historian should govern the pencil of the artist.

Disarmingly straightforward though West's reply was, in one respect it was disingenuous. For in a different voice (more authentically his own) he made the opposite point, perhaps much closer to his personal truth, that the painter's history and the writer's were in fact not in the least analogous; that he was the master of one skill and a hobbling cripple in the other. In a letter to his cousin, Peter Thomson, he apologized for not having written sooner, but the truth of the matter was:

I don't like writeing—its as difficult for me as painting would be to you—every man in his way, I could soon as paint you a description of things on this side of the water. . . . I believe I should have made a figure in South America in the time of the conquest when we find the natives of that country communicated with each other by painting the Images of their Amagina-tions & not in writeing characters to describe them . . . [but since] how writeing is your profession [Thomson was a conveyancer] it will make me happy in now and then receiving a specimen of your great abilities in that way & I will promise you for the future I will endeavour to answer them in either Painting or Scrawling.

For all his formal protestations, then, West was not a reporter in paint, a writer of historical prose.

He was a poetic inventor. He was artful in constructing an image of himself as the unspoiled colonial—intuitive, doggedly empirical, an innocent abroad—since so much of polite London found the image beguiling. In fact, his deviation from the conventions of academic history painting rested on more subtle grounds. He had exposed a serious contradiction in its requirements—both to be strictly faithful to the details of narrative *and* to render them poetically noble by the exercise of the imagination. Through the breach in these incompatible demands, West drove his mighty, painterly, coach and four. The result was *The Death of General Wolfe,* his masterpiece.

From its first conception, West rejected literalism and embraced rhetoric. "Wolfe must not die like a common soldier under a Bush," he wrote. "To move the mind there should be a spectacle presented to raise and warm the mind and all should be proportioned to the highest idea conceivd of the Hero. . . . A mere matter of fact will never produce the effect." Accordingly, throughout the composition, from top to bottom, mere fact is overwhelmed by inspired, symbolically loaded invention. It was this unapologetic hyperbole which set West's painting off so dramatically from the prosaic versions that preceded it, none more painfully feeble than Edward Penny's effort of 1763.

Edward Penny, *The Death of General Wolfe* (1763), detail

Where that product of honest toil conscientiously had the General attended only by two officers and set down in a shrubby clearing apart from the battlefield, West produced the grandiloquent lie the public craved: a death at the very centre of the action; the firing of guns still sounding at his back; the St. Lawrence that he had finally conquered to his right; three groups of officers and men arrayed like a Greek chorus to witness the tragedy.

Of the *dramatis personae* only Monckton, standing at the left, Isaac Barré, leaning over the General from behind, and Hervey Smyth, his aide-de-camp, holding his arm on the left, had played conspicuous parts on the Heights of Abraham. But Monckton, himself badly wounded, was busy in another part of the field at the time of Wolfe's death. Apparently there was a surgeon brought to help stanch Wolfe's three wounds, but it was certainly not the mysterious "Adair" identified as the figure at his right. Nor was the Ranger at the left Captain Howe (of later fame in the American war). But the most startling fiction of all was the Indian, posed in the Antique form of poetic contemplation, precisely the quality commonly denied to the "Savages," as they were invariably called by the British of Wolfe's generation. The General himself had considered them to be irredeemable barbarians, cruel and depraved. What is more they fought, exclusively, for the other side. In fact, it seems likely that the Indian auxiliaries of the

French, concealed in the long grass and corn and picking off individual British soldiers, did more damage to Wolfe's troops than did the French regulars. The bizarre notion that Wolfe would have tolerated their presence at the moment of his apotheosis would have been a bitter jest to anyone familiar with his prejudices.

West's sentiments, on the other hand, were quite different. He had seen the Mohawks employed not as enemies but as allies of the British in Pennsylvania and had idealized them as the embodiments of native nobility. His generation and Wolfe's were separated less by a great span of years than by an immense gap in taste. What the Augustans saw as repellent barbarity, the devotees of *sensibility* thought virile, natural and uncorrupted. West had already painted a genre scene of a Mohawk family, and in his history of Penn's Treaty with the Indians would reiterate this essentially benign view of the relations between the races. So if Wolfe's death were to be designed as a tragic history of Antique grandeur, how better to reinforce it than by making the Indian embody the essence of natural aristocracy in his Michelangelesque torso and noble, even Roman, profile?

There was another reason for the inclusion of these figures at the left: they were there to celebrate America itself; the raw vigour of the New World, a place of buckskin and forest virtues that might supply the necessary power and resources to regenerate a decadent and enervated Europe. Just as the great towering flag of the Union proclaimed the might of the British Empire, the Ranger and the Indian announced (prematurely) its essentially American identity. Together these morally charged insignia turned West's painting into a secular Passion scene, a Lamentation, an icon of the British Empire.

It was, however, an icon that told a story. West borrowed heavily from stage drama (as well as traditional history paintings) to transpose a narrative sequence to the frieze of figures lined up parallel to the picture plane. The eye is meant to read middle and background action right to left, beginning with the elements that made the battle possible—the British fleet anchored on the river, then the action of the dawn of September 13 with field-guns being hauled into place. At the extreme left West records the decisive turning-point of the battle, when the British infantry unloosed the devastating musket volley on the confident, advancing French. From this point the eye turns and travels in the reverse direction left to right, moving with the messenger who brings news of the victory (a figure whom West brought closer and closer to the scene of the central group as he made further copies on commission). The waving hat of the messenger connects with the pointing hand of the Ranger in whose mouth the public, well-versed in Wolfiana, would put the words "They run," said to have been reported to the dying commander. The sash supporting Monckton's wound runs parallel to his left arm, which in turn drops significantly in the direction of Wolfe's own wrist, shattered by the first hit he had taken. On his face with the eyes rolled upwards in both a death agony and the traditional expression of beatific ecstasy, the lips part to utter the lines which in many reported variations thanked God for the news of the victory. Finally, as a kind of dramatic post mortem, the two unidentified soldiers on the extreme right act as mourners with hands clasped and eyes lowered in expressions of reverent prayer.

West also pulled together groups of figures with almost symphonic power and articulation. He confined the background action of the battle to a great diagonal wedge, dimly lit except at the horizon, where a brilliant streak of light hovers above the British ships, their masts puncturing the skyline. The foreground figures are set in three distinct triangular groups, yet they are all enclosed within a larger triangle that has the point of the British flag at its apex and the fallen emblems of the imperial war—Grenadier's hat; Wolfe's musket—running along its base. At the centre of this great mass of forms lie two crucially connected spaces: Wolfe's body contained in a slumping parallelogram or ellipse, and the flag, exactly aligned with it, the billowing fold emphasized by the chiaroscuro of the clouds. The banner thus becomes Wolfe's cross; his saintly attribute; the shroud for his body; and the meaning of his history.

It was a stunning *tour de force* that, in public opinion, all but annihilated the reservations of the dwindling band of critics. The King was sufficiently moved from his initial scepticism to commission a copy from West, who subsequently painted another four for various patrons. For those beyond London and even beyond England who were unable to see the painting, the publisher and cultural entrepreneur Richard Boydell had William Woollett engrave the painting. Though it was an expensive print—perhaps five guineas—the engraving sold in phenomenal quantities. Boydell made his fortune from this single work, netting what, for the eighteenth century, was the staggering sum of £15,000. He went on to become an Alderman and London's most powerful cultural entrepreneur, the publisher of the Shakespeare Gallery. Woollett seems to have been the first engraver to be paid on a royalty basis, so that he too became rich on the back of West's genius, to the tune of £7,000.

As for Benjamin West himself, no less than his subject, he had climbed to the summit of his powers and reputation. He was officially designated court history painter to the King and produced another fifty paintings for the avid

Benjamin West, *The Death of the Earl of Chatham*
(top) and *The Death of Nelson*

George III. But none of them remotely approached the dramatic intensity and sweep of the *Wolfe*. Since one death scene had worked so well (and since the deathbed was a favourite spectacle of late eighteenth-century taste) he tried many more, each feebler than the last. *The Death of Bayard* was a little better than *The Death of Epaminondas,* which in turn was much better than his unfinished and oddly reticent *Death of the Earl of Chatham,* until at last the genre completely collapsed along with its subject in the histrionic failure of *The Death of Nelson.*

It seems likely, though, that this affable and harmlessly conceited man was content enough with his status and wealth not to fret unduly over the fading powers of the Muse. Comfortably ensconced in Panton Square with his wife Betsey and their children, he wrote cheerfully in his atrocious syntax and spelling:

I can say I have been so fare successful in that I find my pictures sell for a prise that no living artist ever received before. I hope this is a circumstance that will induce others to do the same for the great necessity a man is under to have money in his Pokt often distrects the studies of youths contreary to theitr geniuses.

Notwithstanding Reynolds's objections, West remained a pillar of the Academy and in 1792 had the rich satisfaction of actually succeeding his old critic in the presidential chair.

What had he done to Wolfe, his memory, his history? The success of the painting, in all its fanciful inventions and excesses of poetic licence, had been such that when British children of future generations grew up drilled in the pieties of imperial history, it was West's scene they imagined rather than any more literal account. Art had entirely blotted out mere recall, let alone evidence. Two years after the exhibition on the Pall Mall, the marble monument to Wolfe, commissioned as early as 1759, was finally unveiled in Westminster Abbey. The sculptor, Wilton, had also managed to combine allegory and history by having a decorously half-draped Wolfe attended by two officers in contemporary dress, while Fame brings the obligatory laurels and the battle is recorded on bas-relief below. In its genre the monument is an unexceptional and sentimental tribute, and with West's rhetoric imprinted in the popular mind it never manages to become more than a footnote to his achievement.

After West, nothing could dispel the odour of sanctity that lay over Wolfe's memory. When George Townshend published a mordant satire on the monument project around the theme of the Vanity of Human Glory, the Duke of Albemarle was so incensed that he challenged him to a duel, and was prevailed on to desist only by the personal

Benjamin West, *Self-Portrait* (circa 1770)

intervention of Pitt. And while the stars of other imperial conquistadors—Robert Clive, Warren Hastings—fell almost as precipitously as they had risen, Wolfe's remained sempiternally brilliant.

What more could possibly be said?

# 3
# Deep in the Forest

*The Massachusetts Historical Society,*
*November 21, 1893*

It was not quite Thanksgiving. Dead leaves, brown
and papery, piled up against the curbstones; a grey
November light mantled red-brick Boston, and
forty sombre men filed into the meeting room of
the Massachusetts Historical Society on Tremont
Street. It was one of those morally upholstered
places where the Boston Brahmins could defeat
the contradictions of their Puritan legacy by feeling dignified and comfortable at the same time. A
whole day, carefully planned, could be spent
moving from one such *sanctum* to the next: the
Athenaeum for the morning; the St. Botolph Club
for lunch; the Society for the afternoon. The
agreeable consequence was that a Brahmin back-
side would be welcomed only by studded leather
armchairs; a Brahmin sensibility soothed by oak-
panelled walls and unassertive, familiar company;
the Brahmin temper left undisturbed to read,
snore or sniff a weak brandy and water. With the

Brahmin thus sheltered from the incivilities of modern life, the barbarian hordes—plutocrats, democrats, Jews in West Roxbury, Irish in south Boston, and especially women, loquacious, determined, vexing women—might all be safely relegated to the remote horizons of the next century.

For the time being, at least, history if not wholly on their side was at least firmly in their custody. And they had come, this bleak afternoon, to pay tribute to one of the pillars of their temple, now fallen; by common consent, the greatest and the oddest of their company—Francis Parkman. There were ancestral names among them, keepers of the flame, a true priesthood amidst the hard paganism of the modern time: Adamses and Coolidges, Winthrops and Lowells; and only his own manifold infirmities had kept Leverett Saltonstall away. Compared with these tribes of the righteous, the Parkmans had been nothing much—a mercantile fortune; a succession of incvitable Unitarian preachers leavened with the occasional family ne'er-do-well. But Parkman himself had become one of their number as surely as if to the manner born: a Harvard Overseer; the first President of the St. Botolph; a gentleman scholar, rose-grower and anti-feminist; a man whose whole life had been consumed by the historical vocation; in short, one of nature's aristocrats.

His death, at the beginning of the month, in his seventieth year, could hardly have taken the members of the Society by surprise. Parkman had been crippled with arthritis and rheumatism, smitten with failing sight; his strength seemed to have ebbed lately and he had stayed put for the summer at his cottage on Jamaica Pond. Some privately marvelled that with all his sicknesses, he had survived to his three score and ten, and attributed this to an iron determination to complete his great epic of France and England's struggle in North America. But as obvious as Parkman's ill health had been, they had long been accustomed to his figure, upright in the invalid chair, wheeling about the parlours of Boston. Indeed, he had been ill so long, death almost seemed an illogical interruption. So when President Ellis had announced his passing at their regular meeting on November 3, there were many who felt the news with an unexpectedly keen sorrow. Worse, they had to sit through Charles Adams's lengthy report on his experience at the Chicago World's Fair, a phenomenon that Parkman could reliably have been expected to have detested. To general amazement Adams, who like all his family was hard to please, seemed to have been quite taken with the whole thing. There had been, he claimed, a gratifying "spirit of order and decorum . . . a noticeable absence of rudeness or scolding and absolutely no loud language or profanity much less roughness or violence." Even the Babylonian scale of the expense—a shocking thirty million dollars—failed to dim Adams's un-

seemly exhilaration. "Of all the visions of architec-
tural beauty which human eyes have dwelt upon, it
may well be asked if anything can compare or, even
approached the Chicago Fair."

It was fitting, then, that a Special Meeting
should have been called (as President Ellis noted
the event, exceptional in the Society's hundred-
year history) to be dedicated to Parkman's memory. They could expect (and duly got) some funeral
verses from Oliver Wendell Holmes: *"He rests
from toil; the portals of the tomb / Close on the last
of those unwearying hands / That wove their pictured webs."* Members distinguished in historical
letters would, in all likelihood, place their own
prosy wreaths on his bier. But there was to be
something more; something they might anticipate
with great curiosity, even excitement. Ellis had let
it be known that many years before, in 1868, Parkman had confided an autobiographical memoir to
his friend, to be read to the Society only after his
death. Now the moment had come when this might
be shared with his colleagues. Perhaps it would
disclose the mysteries of Parkman's prodigious
craft; his gift of painting in paragraphs, of recreat-
ing the identities of La Salle and Champlain,
Montcalm and Wolfe, of tracking their destinies
through the forests and river valleys of pristine
North America, of giving meaning to their lives
and their deaths. Perhaps they would learn how he
had made history.

To begin with, there was a charmingly self-deprecating preface, evidently added when Parkman had reviewed the memoir. "Running my eye over this paper," he had written, "I am more than ever struck with its *egoism* which makes it totally unfit for any eye but that of one in close personal relations with me." "No, no," came the muffled politenesses in response, and in any event Ellis proceeded. But as he did, it became suddenly, dismayingly apparent that the document *was* indeed saturated, even supersaturated, with egoism, not in the least diminished (in fact reinforced) by Parkman's manner of referring to himself in the third person. Moreover, what they were listening to, with rapidly mounting discomfort, was not history at all but case history. It spoke to them of sickness, torments mental and physical, an unceasing, unsparing war between body and mind; of monstrously self-imposed ordeals, and despair at imagined imperfections. They had known a man who (in all but his work) seemed to them the very epitome of Yankee resilience, stoicism and intellectual toughness. What fell from these pages was the self-portrait of a creature in pain. The great engine of historical creation they had so admired was, he now confessed, a machine horribly out of control, "a locomotive, built of indifferent material under a head of steam too great for its strength, hissing at a score of crevices yet rushing on at accelerating speed to the inevitable smash."

# Deep in the Forest

Was he, then, a Samson Agonistes, whom they had imagined an American Thucydides? Was this poor tragic figure, crumpled in pain and hysteria, the same man whose prose had encompassed the American landscape and had made of the death of Wolfe a great transfiguration? Was this truly Parkman, the historian-as-hero?

*50 Chestnut Street, Boston, February 1880*

It was all the wrong way about. When there was darkness in the streets of Beacon Hill, his brain flooded with light; that brilliant needle-sharp light of the plains; the light that kept him writhing with insomnia. When there was daylight, he had to fortify his north-facing study at the top of the house to keep it away. On mercifully grey mornings he could open the shutters a little, but when a hard winter sun shone the dry radiance irritated his cornea and flooded his eyes with tears. Then there was nothing for it but to close the heavy drapes altogether and work by candlelight. If he then shut his eyes he could listen more attentively, as the girl read documents to him in her fractured Boston-Irish French, comprehending nothing of what she said. Only in his blackness could he make those words live; people his imagination and the Canadian landscape with soldiers and forts, Indians and creaking boats; inscribe into his chronicle utterances and acts, decisions and their consequences. His wisdom had turned owlish; his history nocturnal; his strength rose when others slept.

There were times, now, when he could, if he was very careful, manage a little reading himself; five or ten minutes at a time, followed by as many minutes again of rest. In this way he could, on his best days, his hand shading his brow, complete a whole morning of such staccato work. But there were times too when he overdid it and would collapse into such terrible pain and exhaustion that the Bigelow sisters would have to nurse him back with thin soup and tepid tea. If he avoided these crises it might even be possible to write directly, rather than dictate. He worked with red pencil on orange paper—the combination of colours that seemed least glaring—in a neat, economical hand. But there would be days when his mind was steeled for the exercise but his body conspired against it; when arthritis made it impossible to bend his forearm. On such days he might bring out a contraption he had devised twenty years before to cope with his failing sight. Wires guided his hand across the horizontal lines so that he might actually write with his eyes shut. But the wooden frame to which the wires were attached could also be stood on end, like a small music stand or artist's pad, so that he might work with an arm extended in the manner of a painter.

By such fits and starts, with interruptions and withdrawals, his great chronicle of the encounter of France and England in North America grew, chapter by chapter, volume by volume. His ailments made it an inconceivably laborious process and his working convictions made it more so. For Francis Parkman refused the short cuts offered by secondary sources, almost all of which he despised, as being the pompous adjudications of dull men on other dull men; the "pallid and emasculate scholarship" of which he so often complained. Instead he worked only with primary materials— crates of letters and journals; account books and ordinances—that he had found on his travels in France and England or which his long-suffering friend the good Père Casgrain sent him. Batches of these, organised by chronology and theme, would be read to him over and again until from their scraps and shreds he had sewn together in his mind the splendid fabric of his history. Was there any historian before him, he wondered, who could so well understand the meaning of the word *painstaking*?

The history of this history began long before its writing. For Parkman it had started in childhood, just as Wolfe had accepted his destiny as a soldier's son and a mother's hero. Parkman rebelled against the expectations of his parents, against the suffocating reasonableness of their Unitarianism, the mercantile urbanity they and their kind prized. When early signs of a "fragile constitution" had indicated therapeutic exposure to fresh air, Francis Parkman, Sr., had packed the boy off to his uncle's farm at Medford. From there he had gone roaming in the Fells, wandering into the thick woods of cedars, red oaks and pines, trapping squirrel and chasing woodchuck from their burrows. He was already in search of a pristine America; one not so old perhaps as the pitted red volcanic rock over which he clambered, but an arboreal, wild place of freedom and purity. He could feel it in the springy rug of leaf and moss, smell it in the savoury mould of its generations and regenerations. It was then, he recollected, that he had first imagined writing an American history that would have the forest as its principal character. Later (but not much) he thought the "Old War" of 1756–63, whose history had been blotted out by the self-congratulatory brilliance of the Revolution, might be just such a heroic enterprise. It was, after all, a story that turned on the moment when one kind of world, a culture driven by faith and authority but damaged by dogma and subservience, would be confronted by another whose energies sprang from aggressive, unruly improvisation. France and England, trappers and priests, soldiers and marines, commanders and intendants, bound together in combat, seemed to him material at least as epic as anything recorded in the annals of Greece and Rome. The climax of their encounter, on the Heights of Abraham, was, he imagined, one of those moments in which a whole universe now remote in its values and virtues was reformed into the shape required by modern empires. Wolfe and Montcalm were, then, chivalric figures; incarnations of duty, sacrifice and resolution; doomed, both victor and vanquished, to perish before a world which had brushed those fancies aside.

What was wanting for such a history, Parkman was further convinced, as he sat in Harvard Hall, captive to the interminable lectures of Jared Sparks, was a new voice. It had to be unapologetically American; a voice liberated from the muffled formalism of the British tradition. What could such people, who dwelled amidst fog and soot, and whose apprehension of the sublime was limited by landscapes of rolling hills and grassy vales, what could they know of the forest; of river valleys that cut through gorges atop which immense conifers towered and leaned, enclosing things within their density which Shropshire and Wiltshire could never fathom. Those English voices that sang most sweetly to his ear—Milton and Byron—were lyric, free of the laconic politeness that had so enfeebled the language. Like others of his generation who turned against their Unitarian fathers—Longfellow and Whitman—Parkman too wished to give lyric expression to his exhilaration with the landscape and history, the space and time, of his nation.

To find such eloquence, he already knew, would not be easy. There remained in him enough of his Puritan forefathers to believe that it must be earned through grinding labour and ordeal. Nor would he find what he sought in the library or even the archive, places where the spirit became desiccated. It awaited him somewhere beyond the academy; in the landscape itself.

So his education as a young man filled the spaces where Harvard was not. On every vacation he took himself off with a few companions, sometimes without company, on long, punishing walking expeditions in New Hampshire and Maine; to Lake George and the Notch. In silent river valleys and lakeside clearings he communed with ghostly figures whose hatchets had already cut a path but who had left no tracks and no history other than the rudimentary jottings of a journal; perfunctory lines in a sketch-book. Parkman planned his journeys precisely to recover as far as he could the direct, physical experience of those whose lives he would one day write: spoke to ancient survivors of the Revolutionary war; hunted and pitched tent where he knew the Canadian Jesuits, where trappers and their Indian allies, had stayed; marched along the paths taken by British soldiers towards hapless ambush or brilliant victory.

Sometimes this naïve passion for authenticity, the need to hear a twig break beneath his foot as it had for Champlain or Howe, led him directly to disaster. In his wanderings he fell from sheer cliff paths; sank to his chest in swamp; was eaten alive by clouds of ravenous blackfly; and pitched from his flimsy canoe into the bone-chilling waters of the Magalloway. His body began to record these histories in scars, dislocations, dull muscular aches that in later life would cripple legs and arms.

But Parkman's demanding Muse remained un-deterred. If anything, like that of the Jesuit fathers whose tenacity he would chronicle with grudging respect, his sense of mission fed on these bruising adversities. Not that he seemed unhappy or soli-tary at Harvard. Quite the contrary, he had some-thing of a reputation for gregariousness: a stalwart of the Hasty Pudding and the Chit-Chat Club. Yet, something was longing to break free of undergrad-uate affability. In 1843, in his junior year, he plunged into a black depression explained (as many times afterwards) by the punishments of his physical routines and by bizarre references to chemistry experiments in his youth that he gen-uinely believed had introduced something un-wholesome into his metabolism.

.    .    .

Therapy for his sinister and baffling contamination, as for all young men of his rank and culture, was Europe. But Parkman let it be known that he wanted to avoid the standard route of the Grand Tour, and his writings are full of bored contempt for temples classical and Christian. Instead he opted for what was fast becoming the alternative tour of the Romantic generation—Sicily and Naples, rather than Florence and Rome; the rugged extremities of the country rather than the cultivated centre. In Sicily the young Bostonian drank deep of the "black Falernian wine" and made the obligatory Gothic pilgrimage to the Palermo catacombs. Pushing his way through crowds of beggars, whores and the great tribes of cats (that were, at least, preferable to the rats they were kept to deal with) Parkman descended into the black depths. "Mummies, each from his niche in the wall grinned at us diabolically. . . . Coffins piled up below, men—shrunk to a mere nothing, but clothed as they used to be above ground . . . a row of skulls under the cornices." This was not, he thought, any kind of communing with lost souls; rather an indulgence in the grotesque; a costumed trash collection of the defunct: "children just dead," a few men flung down in a "corner awaiting the drying up process."

He needed other kinds of company. In Rome he oscillated between excesses of sybaritic abandonment (as much as a Yankee could) and excesses of organized self-mortification. The carnival gave him the first; a monastery of the hair-shirted Order of the Passionists, a punishing dose of the latter. In the deafening, dancing tumult of the carnival, Parkman drowned in wine and flowers and became excited as he pelted unattainable women with roses.

To battle with flowers against a laughing and conscious face—showering your ammunition thick as the carriage passes the balcony then straining your eyes to catch the last glance of the blackeyed witch and the last wave of the hand as the crowd closes around her, this is no contemptible amusement.

Aroused by heat and turmoil, Parkman nonetheless remained in thrall to his obsession with America's chilly wildness. As stunning a spectacle as Lake Como, glistening below the Alps, merely ended up reminding him that it was a pale reflection of the unkempt glories of Lake George. Metropolitan Europe was worse. Paris and London, the one devoted to pleasure, the other to commerce, reinforced his prejudice that the great cities were places of moral infection, full of human types whose degeneracy was of a piece with their habitat. In London he went out of his way to harass "some wretched clerk" whose "vacant lobster eyes, nose elevated in the air and elbows stuck out at right angles, a pewter knob of a cane playing at his lip" marked him out as a quarry for the American hunter. Following closely on his heels he frightened the creature into supposing he was being pursued by a criminal, and was then vastly amused by his victim's discomfort.

Evidently Parkman was not, as his parents imagined, destined to be a lawyer. He had another apprenticeship altogether in mind. Between lectures at Harvard Law School he took lessons in bareback riding from a company of circus riders then in Cambridge. This was to give him the skills he imagined he would need on an expedition to the West, following the routes of the waggon trains. There on the prairies he might find his starting point, a world of Indian and buffalo: primitive America, the place from which his histories, wherever they might lead, had to begin.


In the spring of 1846 Parkman set off with one of his Harvard friends and a kinsman whose very name proclaimed his pedigree: Quincy Adams Shaw. From Ohio they went by steamboat to the "jump-off" at St. Louis. In the beginning Parkman rejoiced, much as he had in Sicily, at his release from the starchy civilities of Atlantic culture. But it was not long before all his imagined epiphany with the West decomposed under a brutal sun and the terrifying illimitable space of the prairie. Instead of feeling married to the landscape, he was repelled and threatened by it. The heat was "sultry and almost insupportable"; the immense electrical storms rolling around and around the horizon, horrid, fearsome things; the noble buffalo (when finally sighted) "no very attractive spectacle with their shaggy manes and the tattered remnants of last winter covering their backs in irregular shreds and patches and flying off as they ran"; the cacti hung "like reptiles at the edge of every ravine." The human specimens were not much better: pelt traders living in tents slung with grimy hides, with bloated squaws for company, one memorably described by Parkman as an "impersonation of gluttony and laziness" hidden deep in the recesses of her tepee. Indeed the Plains Indians, so far from embodying the qualities of a natural aristocracy or resisting the arrogant and corrupting intrusions of the average American, appeared to Parkman to display most of the wretchedness of the whites in even more squalid and incorrigible style. Pawnees hated the Crow who mistrusted the Dakota who preyed on the Arapahoe. It was nothing but an endless scavenger hunt in a godforsaken desert.

It was finished before it had begun, then, this romance with the West. He had thought to find some sort of wellspring for America and had discovered instead a barren thing; an antechamber, not of heaven, but of hell. The force of the disenchantment nearly killed him. As the members of the Massachusetts Historical Society heard the memoir reach the Oregon Trail, they listened to a self-portrait of pathetic horror: a man humiliated by incapacity; half-dead with sickness; eaten up with remorse; "reeling in the saddle with weakness and pain." The sun, he thought, had blinded him; his stomach heaved and gagged; his brow dripped with fever. Between a constantly disappearing Valhalla on the western horizon and a retreat back East he was lost, paralysed. Of all the sketches in *The Oregon Trail,* none so much resembles a self-portrait as the jetsam of discarded furniture he saw lying about the prairie trail: "shattered wrecks of ancient clawfooted tables, well-waxed and rubbed or massive bureaus of oak." These were fine great things that had migrated long ago from England, settled in New England, been transported to Ohio or Kentucky and then, under some delusion, dragged West before the "cherished relic is . . . flung out to scorch and crack on the plains."

Parkman returned in a state that swung crazily from manic compulsion to complete prostration. "A wild whirl possessed his brain" (he wrote of himself at this time), joined to a universal turmoil of the nervous system which put his philosophy to the sharpest test it had hitherto known. He was incapable of writing up the Oregon Trail notes; it was done for him by his friends Shaw and Charles Eliot Norton, so that the finished result is even more sardonic, condescending and unsympathetic to the West than would have been the case had he

finished it himself. A year later, in 1848, Parkman
nonetheless determined to begin writing history
with an Indian chronicle—not that of the sorry
remnant he had encountered but the last great
defiance of Pontiac against Anglo-French manip-
ulation. It would be a history in which he could
forget the nightmare of the open plain and take
cover once more in the undergrowth and cool
darkness of the conspiratorial woods. It would be
the first chapter of the great epic of the forest.

The ten years that followed were the best and
worst of his life; the beginnings of a creative
outpouring. Real pain mixed with hysteria; neu-
rasthenic obsession with hypochondria and insomnia. In the midst of a summer heat-wave, he
thought empathetically of three toads in his garden at Jamaica Plain "stewed to death under the
stones where they ensconced themselves." The
family rallied round, did what they could to nurse
him and protect him from himself; they were
thinking of other black strains in the stock—Uncle
George Parkman, whose real estate speculations
were notoriously profitable and who had written extensively on the care of lunatics, had just
recently been murdered by a debtor of his who
also happened to be a Harvard Professor of
Chemistry. Though a legal opinion protested the
conviction on the grounds of circumstantial evi-

dence, parts of the body that had been discovered close to the Professor's laboratory in the Medical School (a building donated by Uncle George) had included false teeth identified as those of the victim.

Yet there was little on Francis Parkman's written pages to suggest a man stranded at the border of his sanity, in the grip of convulsions. Whether dictated or painfully pencilled along the wire guides of his writing frame, the end result was often expansive, thoughtful and elegant, and at times sardonic. Despite the periodic descents into anguish, in writing *The Conspiracy of Pontiac* Parkman believed he had held at bay "The Enemy," as he called the formless beast that stalked his footsteps in and out of the forest of his mind.

And when he felt The Enemy was closing in, there were fresh troops at hand to come to his rescue. In 1850 he met and married Catherine Scollay Bigelow, herself a product of two of Boston's most famous clans. The match could not have been more ideally suited to Parkman's peculiar needs, for her father was a celebrated physician and she a devotee of the northern New England landscapes. It was ultimately on those cold hills and dense woods that the historian had set his sights; a sharp turn away from the western prairies and back to the theatre of the Anglo-French wars.

"His martial instincts were balanced by strong domestic inclinations," Parkman would write of

Wolfe, and as usual, these terms applied equally to himself. Agitated and insecure as he was, somehow Parkman constructed a kind of nest for himself (or rather had it built for him by the women of his family). After his father's death in 1852 they spent the bitter winters in town in the big brick house on Walnut Street and the summer in the leafy suburban village of Milton. In 1853 Francis Jr. was born and though now in the trough of a clinical depression, Parkman managed to rally enough to design and build a fair-season cottage on Jamaica Pond. This was to be the closest to a home that he ever experienced; three acres, a reedy, lily-strewn patch of water on which he rowed, his back to the sun.

The idyll quickly evaporated. In 1857 his four-year-old son died and although a daughter, Katherine, was born the same year, the birth did little to raise his wife from the depths of grief. She herself died in 1858, leaving a new baby, Mary, and her husband now completely lost in a great billowing tide of hysterical wretchedness.

The Enemy seemed to have triumphed after all. Picking up the pieces of this human wreckage, the Bigelows stepped in. Parkman's sisters-in-law came out to the cottage to nurse both father and children; then in the fall shipped them back to Chestnut Street, the house that became the historian's asylum from others and himself. Mother

Harvard, in the guise of the Medical Faculty, stepped in to concern herself with the fate of this lost son. "Displaying that exuberance of resource for which that remarkable profession is justly famed," he later wrote in bitter reflection, ". . . one was for tonics, another for a diet of milk; one counselled galvanism, another hydropathy; one scarred him behind the neck with nitric acid, another drew red hot irons along his spine with a view of enlivening that organ. . . . One assured him of recovery. Another, with grave circumlocution lest the patient should take fright, informed him he was the victim of an organic disease of the brain which must needs dispatch him to another world within twelve month."

After a ghoulish winter in Paris in 1858, Parkman came back to the house on the pond. All he had done in the past decade was a feeble, self-indulgent romantic novel called *Vassall Morton,* but even this kind of creative power had left him in the years of total collapse. Yet groping through the jumbled sequence of darkness and light, there was something, at the end of it all, that beckoned him back to mental order. If almost all his faculties seemed to have defected to The Enemy—his sight, his capacity to walk or write—there was one at least that remained loyal, his sense of smell. Parkman's nose was, in fact, a mighty thing: bold and big-boned and powerfully fleshed-out. It could inhale the fragrance of flowers that must have bathed his distracted brain with pleasure. For *en route* to recovering his life as Parkman the Historian, he became Parkman the Horticulturalist, building first a greenhouse; then growing lilies and roses; then experimenting with new grafts and strains until, finally, he had created an entire realm of flowers. Perhaps he recalled that earlier carnival battle in Rome when he had hurled blooms at girls on balconies. As his horticulture flourished so life gradually returned. He published *The Book of Roses* in 1861; became more famous as a gardener than a historian; was appointed Professor of Horticulture at Harvard; and gradually, hesitantly, from his garden path, approached again the forbidding immensity of the woods.

And then, from the mid-1860s, he entered their history. The summers were usually given over to the world of the pond; the winters in the study at Chestnut Street, to *France and England in North America*. Box after box of documents came from his archivist friends in Paris and Canada. Sometimes he felt strong enough to travel and gather his own documents that would be shipped back to Boston. The ponderous routine of being read to, of dictating, of having his own work read back and refined and edited, began. The Enemy now put in only an occasional appearance, usually during the long, merciless nights of his insomnia. But given a soft grey morning light, Parkman could proceed again, a few minutes at a time, to his business.

Francis Parkman

Others were going blind in Boston in the service of Clio: Prescott, the great chronicler of the Conquests, most famously. But Parkman had evolved into a craftsman whose energies were pinpointed into minute detailed tasks. He had become a stitcher of tapestry, albeit with slowness, like those at Bayeux who had chronicled another encounter between France and England; Norman power and Saxon bloody-mindedness. As in such a tapestry, there were brilliantly fabricated moments, flights of pure fanciful embroidery, stitched into the epic. But when he and others could stand back and look at the thing, unfolding before them, the marvel of it all was unmistakable.

And now it was almost done. The previous summer he had gone to Quebec once more to see the grassy field at the Heights of Abraham; to stand at the face of the cliff and imagine again the daunting ascent, the sheer improbability of it. The time had come to deliver Wolfe to his consummation and Montcalm to his, surely a symmetry of providential design (however much his ingrown doubt rebelled against any such nonsense). Perhaps, though, all his own trials were in some measure a preparation that he could better understand the compulsive, perfervid intensity of the General. He wrote of Wolfe:

When bound on some deadly enterprise of war he calmly counts whether or not he can compel his feeble body to bear him on till the work is done. A frame so delicately strung could not have been insensible to danger; but forgetfulness of self and the absorption of every faculty in the object before him, shut out the sense of fear. . . . His nature was a combination of tenderness and fire. . . . He made friends readily and kept them and was usually a pleasant companion though subject to sallies of imperious irritability which occasionally broke through his strong sense of good breeding. For this his susceptible constitution was largely answerable for he was a living barometer and his spirits rose and fell with every change of weather.

At the supreme crisis of his life, with his army withering away, Wolfe

lay in an upper chamber, helpless in bed, his singular and unmilitary features haggard with disease and drawn with pain; no man could less have looked the hero. But as the needle, though quivering, points always to the pole, so through torment and languor and the heats of fever the mind of Wolfe dwelt on the capture of Quebec.

Past and present dissolved at this moment. He became Wolfe and Wolfe lived again through him; the man's perseverance and fortitude; the punishments of his body; the irritability of his mind; the crazy, agitated propulsion of his energies all flowed between subject and historian; overtook and consumed him, robbed him of sleep and colonized his days so that the writing of it all, the remembering, the recitation drove him on, relentlessly, became akin to and part of the hard, forced climb upwards to the heights; the drum-measured advance across the field, unstoppable till the very finish.

# 4
# On the Heights of Abraham

*Nine a.m., September 13, 1759*

An ill day for a battle we thought, hard to see our
enemy with the wet mist hanging on the hill be-
twixt us and them and the rain falling. When the
low sun appear'd it shone straight in our eyes as we
faced the town where the French were musterd in
front of the walls. So at the start we heard more
than we saw, first their drums and the clatter of
some pieces and the low sound of men beginning
their march. The General knew we were as much
afraid as any men in such a position, who could
have no way back and were held from going forward, so he came along the line to us and spoke
some words to help our resolve and keep us still
until it was time to fire.

We were tried, God knows, for as they came
closer, the first musket shots came, cracking and
hissing through the air and amidst the long grass,
and from behind the cover of trees to our right we
could make out Indians coming closer, some of
them creeping on their bellies. Some of our men

fell to their shot without ever making a move, like tin soldiers at a midsummer fair, and this gall'd us so our hands trembled and shook at our muskets with mixd fear and rage, the more when we heard the Savages whooping and yelling. Then we made out the grey uniforms of the French coming at us at a trot and yelling and singing that they supposd us turning tail at the sight of them. If God's truth be told we damn'd nearly did so for directly behind me, a fellow dropp'd his musket and crumpled on the ground and cried in a low way he was shot before he stoppd squirming and was at peace. And I heard others about me swear and pray and another set up a little moaning under his hat, for we could now see them very plain two hundred yards, no more, coming at us, some breaking into a run then dropping for cover and advancing again. It was an irregular jerky movement like tongues of fire darting hither and thither but all in our direction.

Still we held our pieces and the General himself he showed us his face and he was smiling an odd smile and holding his arm up and I could see his other hand had been shot away for there was blood on the sleeve of his fresh coat. And I could hardly bear to keep from going off for that flowing liquid feeling poured through my bowels and my heart banged inside my breast. No more than a hundred paces maybe and we could see their own faces now, their wigs all dirty and their run a kind of drunken stumble. Out of the corner of my eye I just saw Wolfe shout and drop his sword, the flash of it in the sun and the whole line barked out its volley; and we were sheltered in the great noise and smoke and smell of powder and dropp'd down to reload while the fellows at our backs let off their shot. We had done this so many times down below on the islands till it seemd a cloddish piece of obedience but now it servd us well as the volleys came so close together they made one great hellish thunder over and over again, echoing inside our heads and making our eyes swim and our throats choke. And when all that working and tamping and discharging were done and Mr. Monckton ordered the cease, the silence seemed to come from a great hole we had torn in the body of their army. For as the light came through the smoke and the din faded, we could hear terrible screaming and saw the slaughter we had done and their backs running to the town. The Highlanders began their shouting and with a skirl of pipes set after the French their broadswords out, but I was glad we didnt follow for I had little stomach for it.

Then up comes the Captain and tells me to take a message to the General to say our line had held and the enemy was put to flight. And I had rather it had be another man; I was tired at all we had done last night and this morning. But I obeyed and ran over the field stepping through blood and faces upturned in death and a few horses, poor beasts their bellies all spilld open. But the General was nowhere that the Brigadier had said, nor wherever I looked and I was making to go back down our line when I suddenly saw him, lying on a mound beside a sorry little bush attended by just two men, one leaning over and supporting Wolfe with his arm. Mr. Browne, for that was his name, was begging him to lie and shouted at me to come fast and help. I approached Wolfe and saw his face had gone stiff and greenish and his red hair glistened with sun and sweat. Blood had matted his belly where another ball had struck him and now more was oozing through his shirt and coat, so seeing he would not live I told him our news and in a groaning, gurgling sort of way I could hear him praise God for it.

Katherine Lowther to Mrs. Henrietta Wolfe:

Madam,

Only this morning ye tidings of ye Dreadful Calamity reached me & I yield to the first impulse to mingle my grief with that of the Hero's Mother at the loss of One who whatever his Worth to his Country was to us both doubly precious. I am aware, Madam, of the Chasm between us which has not been heal'd. Your displeasure at yr Noble son's partiality to one who is only too conscious of her own Unworthiness has cost her many a Pang. But you cannot without cruelty still attribute to me any Coldness in his Parting for, Madam, I always felt & express'd for You both reverence and Affection & desir'd you ever first to be consider'd. Yet our hearts are now too deeply wrung for reproaches.

I have only humbly to express ye Wish that any Messages which he may have left for me and which may have been entrusted to ye Bearer of his private Effects may Thro your Indulgence, Madam, be forwarded here to me. There was a Picture of me which I know it was His wish should in case of Fatality, come again into my Hands. May God comfort you, Madam, in your great affliction is the constant Prayer of

Your sincere Humble Servant

K. Lowther

Raby Castle,
October 25th 1759

## *Two*

# Death of a Harvard Man

Gu N Briggs

# 1
# Honest Sweat:
# The Blacksmith's Son

Miserable Heathen!

I want to ask you one question, Why do you want to have Professor Webster hang, I can think of nothing else than this that you want only to gratify your thirst for Blood. If Professor Webster hang you will meet with a terrible death, one that you little dream of. You have had one man hung and I should think that was enough for one month. Can you see those poor daughters and wife of Professor Webster pleading for him without taking pity on him. From Maine to Louisiana there has been petitions you have turned a deaf ear, there is a band forming in the city under my command who on the 25th of this month (if Professor Webster is hung) will burn your dwelling to the ground and put an end to your damnable life; you are the most hard-hearted man I ever heard of. You are a God damned miserable lying, thieving villainous rascal—a nice man for a Governor.

A nice man indeed. George Briggs sighed wearily and tossed the shrieking letter at the growing pile on his mahogany desk. Him, a heathen, who had laboured the best part of his life to bring together the service of the state and the ministry of Christ! Him, hard-hearted, who had begun his career in the law defending a poor savage Indian against the rope. But even these were not the worst that had been said of him. Another such ranter had written: "Murderer thou art and murderer thou shalt yet confess thyself to be though thy hands may not have been wet with human blood." Did these lost souls truly imagine he took pleasure in upholding the severest decree of the law? Did they not comprehend that so far from usurping the place of God, he was but the obedient instrument of blind and impartial justice? He had told them, had he not, how it would have given him "unspeakable pleasure" to have set the execution aside, if only for the sake of the Professor's prostrate family. But in good conscience, before God, he could not and would not.

And as the appointed day drew close, the din (for he could hear these voices as if they were shouted in his face) grew louder. It was as if one of his Baptist prayer meetings had become possessed by demons, all the more cunning for speaking in tongues, some of them a horrible mockery of the evangelist: "Set thy house in order for thou shalt die and not live." "Cain! the voice is calling to thee, 'where is thy brother?'" "Dear Fellow Sinner bound with me to the Judgement Seat of Christ. I inform you that I am innocent of the blood of Professor Webster and also to let you know that all who are engaged in making laws for this Commonwealth and thereby condemning to Death their fellow subjects cannot escape the Damnation of Hell."

Other voices were no more agreeable for sounding a different note. Could there really be such a person as "Little Fanny of the South"? Were it not for the Charleston postmark he would have suspected a hoax. In a simpering ingratiation no less revolting coming as it did from a child, this Fanny implored him to commute the sentence. "Oh kind Mr. Governor you cannot imagine my feelings when I read that Dr. Webster was going to be hung and leave his wife and four little children all alone in this world; for I dont think they will have friends after their Papa is a murderer. But do you really think he intended to kill Dr. Parkman! I do not think so and now kind Mr. Governor do let me beg you not to hang Dr. Webster for you do not know how sorry I feel. Oh! I think it must be an awful death. I wont let Papa know anything about this letter."

Still they came: sober petitions; wild looping scribbles on coarse paper; tiny, sinister script that looked as though a bug had tracked a pin across the page; blue sheets with newsprint cuttings pasted to them and a threatening, single, prophetic name — "Miriam" or "Nehemiah" — signed at the foot. They came from physicians in Erie County, Pennsylvania; from fashionable ladies of New York "on behalf of suffering humanity"; from a gentleman who claimed acquaintance having followed him along the railroad track one evening when the locomotive broke down between Lawrence and Boston; from women reporting Webster's innocence revealed in mesmeric trances; from James Robbins of Pittsfield, Briggs's home-town, who disconcertingly insisted that "they ought to shoot the condemned man and not hang him for God has Told Me So" (God apparently also told him that "men should travel on the Rail Road with Horses and not by Steam," something with which Briggs sometimes had sympathy): "for we are to be one Family All Over the World Soon and Every Man Set under his own vine and Fig Tree with No-one to Molest Him or Make Him Afraid for God has Told Me So."

Fortunate soul to be in such reliable communication with the Almighty! The Governor glanced behind him at his blackthorn stick leaning against the wall of the Corner Office. It had been fashioned, so he had been told, from a shepherd's crook at Delphi beneath the very shade of Parnassus. No oracles here, though, not in the "Athens of America." He took off his silver-mounted spectacles and set them on the green leather desk-top. They were by far the grandest thing he wore, but nonetheless the product of honest toil. A youthful mechanic had given them to him in innocent appreciation many years ago, and he had thought it (and still did) churlish to decline. He rubbed the bridge of his nose and ran a hand through his sandy hair. The saturated heat of the Boston summer raised beads of sweat on his brow and cheeks that ran in tiny rivers down his clean chin and into the black stock knotted about his neck. Even this proclaimed his place among the common sort, for he made a point of refusing to wear a collar with the scarf. He thought, fleetingly, of his blacksmith father in Adams, out in the Berkshire hills, and of Longfellow's celebration:

> *His brow is wet with honest sweat,*
> *He earns whate'er he can,*
> *And looks the whole world in the face,*
> *For he owes not any man.*

Was not Longfellow a colleague of Webster's at Harvard? A pity he had not persuaded the Professor of those Georgic virtues! Brought back sharply from sunny childhood to sombre present, the Governor's features settled into an anxious frown. It was not an expression the people of Massachusetts expected from George Nixon Briggs, for they knew him, surely, as the most amiable of men; their pastor and friend as much as the steward of the Commonwealth. *Great in Goodness* would be the title of a biographical memoir, and without being unctuous he had never made any secret that he supposed simple virtue to be the essence of righteous authority. His devotion to the common good—to Irish orphans whom he wanted to see in common school, stinking drunks whom he would rescue for the great cause of Temperance, freed slaves whom he helped house, hardened criminals whose crooked ways he yearned to make straight—all this was of a piece with his faith. Born a second time into the love of Christ, he was convinced there was no spotting so deep it could not be washed clean in the blood of the Lamb.

His whole bearing proclaimed this belief. Rosy-complexioned and with the erect posture of the Berkshire countryman, George Briggs gave off an aura of invincible wholesomeness, as though he were made of fresh-baked bread. This was itself remarkable in the Boston of 1850, but the reputation jarred badly with the dirty work his office had called him to and from which he could not swerve. John Winthrop's shining City on the Hill had become a swarming, crawling, bursting place season by season. Great riches and great squalor, virtue and crime had made their abode there side by side, but the work of virtue had been detained in the arrest of crime. Marshal Tukey had filled his jails with wretches, and still the whores congregated on Anne Street; the grog shops and alleys slopped about with human refuse—the unrepentant, the murderous, the abandoned—breeding debauchery and cholera. His unhinged accuser was right; hangings would not put an end to killings, but what choice did he have? With the deepest misgivings he had indeed sent the imbecile Daniel Pierson to execution for killing his wife. And the year before, the poor negro Washington Goode had been hanged for a crime of passion. Could he now flinch when a Professor of Harvard College, neither black nor idiot, had committed a crime quite as vile?

Well, it was an affliction and no mistake, a rod across his back. He pushed the big leather chair back from the desk, stood up and stared disconsolately out of the window onto Boston Common. The elms spread their heavy shade over small boys bowling hoops and governesses walking their charges towards the Public Garden, the city's latest amenity redeemed from the mud of the Charles Basin. Rings of blue smoke hung in the air above the "Smokers Circle" graciously provided by Mayor Quincy* for the gasping souls who had recently been prohibited by ordinance from lighting up their cigars on the sidewalk. Somewhere at the foot of Park Street there was an organ-grinder with a marmoset that capered about clutching a tin

*It was Josiah Quincy, Sr. (1772–1864; mayor of Boston, 1823–1828), who supplied this and many other conveniences to the city; he subsequently became President of Harvard (1829–1882). His son, Josiah Quincy, Jr. (1802–1882), was mayor of Boston from 1845 to 1849.

can, right in the shadow of the Old Burial Ground and the Tremont Temple. Improperly for a Baptist, he secretly rejoiced in all these Bostonian proximities, the playful and the worshipful jostling together. He longed to free himself of his black coat and his official politenesses and scamper back to the farm at Pittsfield where he could sit astride his ancient horse, Billy, or stand in the barnyard with doves on his head and arms pecking gently at the proffered grain. Right now the trout would be leaping in the Housatonic, and he owed them his presence, wading into the green water. He had done enough here. He would decline the nomination next year. The anonymous hand that had written at the foot of newspaper cuttings pasted on blue paper "I would like to see you get another vote of mine" would be denied the pleasure of withholding it.

But there was still this bad business to be got behind him before he could pack his bags for the farm. Even at this last stage, a commutation was possible—by his hand alone. But he could see no right way to it. Only one letter from the pile nagged at him, though every instinct he had acquired since taking up the law in Lanesboro those many, many years ago told him it was a spurious confession. He went back to the desk, shuffling in the pile of papers till he found the curling, obsessive hand.

## Honest Sweat: The Blacksmith's Son

Cincinnati, August 18th

I hope your highness will excuse the liberty I have taken if such it may be termed in addressing an entire stranger but my head aches and my brain is on fire so that I know not what I am about, but to the point at once. I understand through the newspapers that Professor Webster is to be hung on the 20th of this month and I wish to say to you that if such be the fact and that he is hung at the appointed time he will be hung an innocent man. He had no more to do with the killing of Parkman than you did—perhaps you may think it very strange that he did not do it but it is nevertheless true for the one that is now addressing you is the one that laid him low.

Yes, yes, folly and lies, fairy tales and fables. But where lay the truth, the real history of George Parkman and John White Webster? Much as he respected the stern proceedings of the trial, he was too much of a lawyer himself (or perhaps too much of a smithy's son) to imagine that it told the whole story. The defence, after all, had opened with one account and closed with another—a fatal strategy; even the prisoner's own confession could not wholly be credited. Indeed, confessions were two a penny; letters had come from states and territories from California to the Carolinas, their writers purporting to have done the deed. In Washington, Texas, some person called Weeks had even written a letter to the *New Orleans Delta* insisting on his own guilt. Briggs understood this epidemic of confession well enough. Had he not heard something like it, God forgive him, at his Baptist meetings when sinners competed with each other to testify, to shout their wickednesses so that they might be redeemed, their sins washed clean in the Jordan waters?

Well, perhaps there was more complicity to be shared in the guilt of John Webster. His hand had killed, and he would be struck down for it. But what of the world that had fathered him and his misdeed? How would it get its quittance? Up and down Beacon Hill and beyond through the West End and over the river in the leafy streets of Cambridge, gentlemen of Harvard were impatient to be rid of this squalid embarrassment, this dreadful reproach to their claims of moral ascendancy. To be sure, they could hardly be implicated, at however many removes. But despite this self-evident truth, the Governor found himself surrendering to twinges of unworthy vexation on their account. He remembered his own address to the College on the inauguration of President Everett; his own steadfast admiration for all it had been and all it promised. When asked about his own education, he took pleasure in the smiling reply, "Three years in a hatter's shop," and that was the truth of it. But it was no secret that he also envied the blessed youths of the Yard; the nobility of the learning supplied for them; their easy assumption that even the most inattentive exposure to godly learning made of them a caste appointed to rule. He had taken them at their word; had broken bread at their tables and joined their causes; had admired their high minds and their fastidious deportment. Doubtless it was unjust to feel so, but George Briggs could not help but feel disabused.

*Had they fallen, then, the Elect?* There were still righteous men amongst them. Old John Quincy Adams, whom the Governor revered, had died but a few years back. And the emancipation cause had fired a new zealotry among such as Phillips and Sumner. It gave him no pleasure to think of those men of fire and fanaticism as the true heirs of the Puritan covenant. Yet those young men were perhaps bound to stir themselves against the mealy-mouthed comfortable theology of Unitarianism: its reassuring convergence of intellect and faith; its rejection of anything not understood by reason. No wonder the oligarchs of the city and the College had been so undefended against the passions, so undernourished with this watery soup of a theology. Dear God, was not Webster a congregant of Francis Parkman's Unitarian church in the North End? And did that fellowship stay his hand, even stir his conscience?

It was a flimsy fence to stand against wickednesses great and small, he thought, and if it had sufficed the men of Harvard College, it was not enough for Boston's great ills. The Governor went again to the open window and caught the freshness of a marine breeze blowing in from the muddy harbour. Down there the Irish were landing, day after day, in their thousands and tens of thousands; unwashed multitudes, raised in poverty and hunger and cruelty and ignorance, now packed together in the tenements of Fort Hill, the North End and the South Cove. Cholera washed through those places like a rank tide. Thousands had perished from the plague just last year. No wonder they take shelter in their idolatrous confession, clean contrary to the refined sensibilities of Beacon Hill and Cambridge. How many *gentlemen* walk in Half Moon Alley or at the back of Hanover Street, even with a handkerchief to their nose, he wondered?

But the Common was green and placid and led Briggs to historical irony. A Puritan city, founded by fugitives from Popery, was now overrun by a new generation of fugitives obstinately loyal to Rome! What kind of world would they father in tight, waterlocked Boston? It would not, he imagined, be one where a new Winthrop would care to pitch his tent. A historic moment was passing. A death had happened; another would follow as a consequence, but the alterations would not end there. A warrant had been made out against a whole class of men whose ruling pedigree went back to the Pilgrims. The raving Millerites had prophesied the end of the world this mid-century year. Well, it looked as though it might be the end of *a* world, at any rate.

He thought of the Parkmans in particular and their pilgrimages and progresses. Even old Ebenezer preaching the Word in his rustic parish at Westborough had shown signs of unbecoming grandeur, keeping a negro servant and having himself styled "the first Bishop of the Church of Westboro" on his tombstone. But his ambitions were null compared to those of his son Samuel, who had begun as tavern boy in the Bunch of Grapes and ended as the baron of Bowdoin Square. His estate was immense; his ships full of China tea and Russian furs; his person draped in blue velvet that parted to reveal a diamond brilliant that dazzled his admirers.

Providence decreed there should be a falling-off. Samuel's daughters, who themselves had married wealth, now lived in the mansion at Bowdoin Square, but his offspring had in their several ways been visited by sorrow and scandal. The namesake, Samuel Junior, was a scoundrel who had fled from the disclosure of a forgery and lived in scarlet, shameless sin somewhere in the pagan sunlight of the Mediterranean. Francis, the Unitarian pastor of the New Church on Hanover Street, was prey to melancholy, a friend to all manner of men in the city and the College but, it was said, a stranger to his own son who had inherited his sickness without his faith. And, God forgive him to think ill of the murdered, but George, a worthy citizen and full of good works, had been known to turn flinty and unyielding where matters of money were concerned.

*Pecunia radix omnium malorum est.* Gold, Boston's shame and Boston's glory; gold lying in the vaults of the great city banks where it lay breeding more money; funds to feed the appetite of the traders and shippers and builders and brokers; gold encrusted on the furnishings of the mighty and even coating the plate or embellishing the porcelain of the most extravagant of their society; gold pressed into the inscriptions of old charters and arms; gold shining from the crown of the lion that yet stood rampant on the roof of the British State-house. And still not enough gold to hand around, so Bostonians had begun to take ship for California where, it was said, it lay on the very ground waiting for the biggest fools to stumble over. They would stumble and find and still be fools. His was not a popular view, though, he knew. The author of *Our First Men* was more in touch with the common view. What had he written? "It is no derogation, then to the Boston aristocracy to say that it rests upon money. Money is something substantial. Everybody knows this and feels it. Birth is a mere idea which grows every day more and more intangible."

Such foolishness, such vanity. How much better

to be the Commonwealth's First Servant and Citizen than a "First Man" (if their priority were measured in hundreds of thousands of dollars). But, he knew, the world thought otherwise. For the pride of money George Parkman had turned wrathful, and for want of it John Webster had turned homicidal. The Doctor had lost his moderation; the Professor, his mind. For what was this crime in its essence but the lowest kind of sordid quarrel over money? Just such a dirty business as could be found in the back streets of the North End. Helplessly, he imagined the two Harvard men locked in violent contention amidst the debris of their learning, leather volumes and glass crucibles flying this way and that.

One dead; another to join him. He would not go to the prison that morning. He had seen too much dying where it did not belong. Against his will he recalled the dreadful figure of Judge Bouldin dropping onto the floor of the House of Representatives in Washington in the midst of announcing another member's death, the judge's wife's terrible cries from the gallery. Nor could he ever forget seeing a poor negro slave seated at the foot of a mast on the Alexandria steamer, his wet, black face brilliantly illuminated as a bolt of lightning struck him and the big ship ploughed on through boiling waters to the dock. He knew, Heaven pardon him, that the blood of Massachusetts men had soaked the red earth of Mexico for a cause he despised but for which he had to provide loyal supply; its author, President Taylor, was dead now, too.

What reprieve could there be?

An usher in black vest and shirt-sleeves brought in yet another pile of letters. The first the Governor saw was made up like an invitation.

Dear Sir,

The undersigned begs the pleasure of your company on Friday morning August 30th at No. 5 Leverett Street to witness a murder. A dish of tea will be taken with the awful ceremony.

Yours with suffocation,

# 2

# Income: The Pedestrian

*Friday, November 23, 1849*

The lettuce sat in its brown bag, wilting in the unseasonable warmth. By the time that the grocer, Paul Holland, got up the courage to investigate the bag's contents, the damage had been done. The leaves had gone flabby, pale and dry. He took the bag from the counter and set it on a cool shelf at the back of the store in the hope it might freshen into resurrection. Such a sorry waste and so unlike Dr. Parkman! He glanced at the wall clock: five o'clock, three hours since he had marched in in that brisk, clockwork fashion of his. The pleasantries had been, as usual, sparse, and about the weather. Sugar (thirty-two pounds) and butter (six pounds) had been ordered for delivery to his house in Walnut Street. The lettuce (bought elsewhere and dearly, for a salad in November was an extravagance) was set down on the counter. He would be back "in a few minutes" he had said, a few minutes. What Dr. Parkman said, he meant, as many a tenant of his had cause to recall. And regular, my

Dr. George Parkman as he last appeared walking the streets of Boston.

goodness, you could set your watch by him; there never was such a man for promptness.

He had left the store on the corner of Blossom Street, walking smartly in the direction of the Harvard Medical College, the hulking, square, red-brick building that squatted with its front in North Grove Street and its rear against the mudflats of the Charles River. A number of people had seen him on the way, his angular, sternly dressed body leaning forward as though his torso were impatient with his legs for not keeping pace. Two schoolboys were trading twelve-year-olds' confidences in the street as the Doctor flew by. This would have been ten to two, Martha Moore surmised at the trial, since she had leaned out of her window and told her young George and his friend Dwight to get themselves to afternoon school sharpish. They had scurried off across the street and up Beacon Hill, arriving just a minute before the dread sentence of "tardy" was ro corded in the roll. Just seventy feet away from the College door, a cart full of a delivery of pig iron castings was being unloaded and weighed by the Fuller brothers in front of their West Boston Iron Foundry. They too remembered seeing the Doctor pass in the midst of their clattering and heaving, heading swiftly up North Grove Street.

Thus, Dr. Parkman entered the building he liked to call "a piece of the Holy Land." Did he emerge again? Some believed it must have been

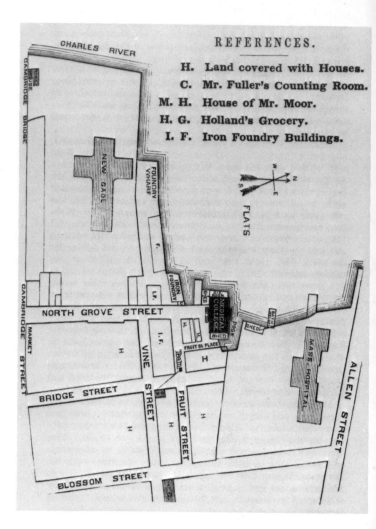

The Harvard Medical College and surrounding streets

so, for they saw him at different times that Friday afternoon cutting a swathe through the Thanksgiving crowds, his stovepipe hat before, his frock coat tails flying aft. A clerk in the Registry of Deeds saw him in Causeway Street; a grocer saw him at the top of the West End in Court Street; an ex-tenant saw him in the centre of town near Milk Street in mid-afternoon. As the sunset was drawing on, Mrs. Abby Rhoades and her daughter Mary, who had been shopping for wool muslin, passed him in Green Street, where he folded himself in two in a deep, polite bow.

Could all these people have been deluded? It was not as if George Parkman was easily swallowed up in a throng. His bustling presence was a fixture on the streets of Boston just because it seemed to proclaim his eccentricity; his public determination to announce "Know ye who I am; of what I am made." Making a point of neither keeping a horse nor taking a carriage, he walked everywhere, collecting his own rents, inspecting his buildings, even, as the Universalist paper the *Trumpet* noted, doing "what some proud but poor men refuse to do, carrying bundles in his hands or under his arms to his own house." He was, in short, the paper concluded triumphantly, a *Pedestrian,* and wore his pedestrianism like a coat of arms. Rather too many times he told the story (bizarre but true) that his only reprimand at Harvard had been for "excessive walking on the Sabbath."

Oliver Wendell Holmes, the Dean of the Medical College, turned these habits into a portrait of the perfect Yankee: exacting yet philanthropic; wealthy yet austere. "He abstained while others indulged, he walked while others rode, he worked while others slept." For those who believed that a physique and physiognomy announced the man within (and a great many in New England did), Dr. Parkman was a fine vindication. For he was all bones and sinew, with no cushion of fat on him to suggest much in the way of genteel ease or languor. His face, with its long nose and pointed chin pulled forward by an underbiting jaw, looked as though it had been sharpened into the shape of the crescent moon, a lean, Yankee Punchinello. It was a face that spoke of direction and urgency like the face of a ticking watch. For time, after all, was the Yankee's capital, placed in his hands by a watchful Providence. It was not something to be frittered away on vanities, but demanded husbanding, investing, spending only where it could bear the rich fruit of interest. And Dr. George Parkman, as all who knew him recalled, was one of God's walking chronometers.

Seen sideways on, George Parkman appeared two-dimensional, all points and principles, a lean, long-shanked man of means. This was the way in which the chronicler of *Our First Men* catalogued him. Worth: $500,000; "bred a physician but practices as a speculator in real estate; owns a vast many

cheap built tenements let at high rates and as he is
his own rent collector and keeps no horse is seen
moving through the city."

But this crude caricature scarcely did justice to
the wonderful strangeness of the Doctor, for the
"speculator in real estate" was also a man of passions
and mysteries, medical, literary and zoological. For
two days in bitter February 1834, he had worked
with John James Audubon, coats off, desperately
attempting to suffocate a golden eagle with charcoal
and sulphur fumes so that the ornithologist might
sketch it without plumage disfigured by the gun or
the knife. But while the thick, yellow vapours sent
the men choking and rushing for the door, the great
bird sat erect on its perch, its eyes glinting, body
defiantly and resolutely alive. Despairing of any
other solution, father and son Audubon resorted to
the usual execution; one tethered the bird's talons
and wings while the other stabbed at its heart. What
had begun as rational, ended in hysteria; what began
as mercy, ended in murder.

This was not the end, though. If Audubon was to
have his sketch he had to get to work before the
rigor mortis set in. So he commenced immediately,
trying to breathe life into his drawing, sweating by
the fire or shivering as the embers died. After five
days of this labor he became sick and crazy with the
effort; he took to his bed, tortured with guilt at
what he had done. Parkman, who was managing
the Boston subscription for Audubon's great vol-

umes, felt doubly responsible as partner and doctor to the "Woodsman of America." Mrs. Parkman nursed him back to health with pots of tea, bowls of chowder and liberal small talk.

He knew all about human frailty, did Parkman, and the way in which from some twisted root it grew into a great trunk of disorder and proliferated branches and twigs throughout the body and mind. His family, after all, was full of such bolting growths. He himself had been drawn to medicine as a way of dealing with all of the infirmities he had experienced as a boy. What did that fool who had scribbled *Our First Men* know of such things! He had not been "bred" a physician, but had made himself into one by hard labour and stubborn determination. One morning in Harvard Medical College the renowned Dr. Rush of Philadelphia came to speak to the students, and Parkman remembered him beginning thus: "Gentlemen I rise from my seat to beseech you—arrest disease in its early stages!"

The arrest of disease! That would be his way, his godly vocation.

But he was not yet sure where or how to concentrate his efforts. Europe would show him, but in a fashion undreamed of by American youths who embarked on pilgrimages in search of the classical ideal. In 1811 Parkman sailed for France on the USS *Constitution*. He reached Paris at the imperial zenith, a city that flattered itself on being the new Rome: virile, benevolent and invincible. An arch was being constructed at its western end that would recall, but supersede, that of Trajan. The horses of Saint Mark and the Madonnas of Bellini had been made over as French. Every day saw some new fantasy realised in costumes of velvet and gossamer, sauces of cognac and cream, buildings of marble or spun sugar.

Such refinements were not for George Parkman of Boston. Through the good offices of the American Minister, Joel Barlow, he was introduced to that living embodiment of Gallo-American cordiality, the Marquis de Lafayette, whose manners and intellect could pass for heavyweight in imperial Paris. But it was at a more improbable table that Parkman found his mentors. In the pretty suburb of Auteuil, where Ben Franklin had held court in the reign of the fat, fated Louis XVI, a different Benjamin had planted his flag. This, however, was no patriot, but Benjamin Thompson, the notorious Loyalist who had begun his career in the same Boston dry goods store as George's father, but had metamorphosed into "Count Rumford" (a pumpernickel pedigree), inventor, landscape gardener and social engineer. Thompson/Rumford now lorded over the villa that had once belonged to Antoine Lavoisier, the greatest of the old regime's chemists, a man of humanity and intelligence who had been guillotined as a tax farmer in the Terror. In a house filled with the broken optimism of the scientific enlightenment, Parkman stood by as Thompson's restless inventiveness buzzed and whirred, concocting the perfectly nutritious soup (at lowest possible cost) for the indigent, the most elegant urban park, the perfectly mechanised water closet—projects of mental and corporeal health put into mutually sustaining balance.

This was more to Parkman's liking than Paris modes. Chez Rumford he encountered the luminaries of the Institut: Destutt de Tracy, Cabanis, Cuvier, men whose sagacity and public-spiritedness advertised the Napoleonic commitment to the empire of ideas as well as arms (or at least their utility). One man of sombre appearance and high moral deportment struck him as especially superior. This was Philippe Pinel, doctor to the insane at Bicêtre and Salpêtrière. Not many men whose appointment dated from the height of the Jacobin Terror had survived into the empire (when a Habsburg princess shared Bonaparte's throne), but the lustre of Pinel's reputation blotted out this embarrassment of chronology. For when learned men, subscribing members of the academies in Metz and Bordeaux and Caen and those other imperial French cities—Rome and Amsterdam and Hamburg—thought of Philippe Pinel, they imagined the one scene that had vindicated the rumoured marriage of science and humanity: the Doctor entering the dank, screaming prison of Bicêtre, with its smells of terror and piss, the insane manacled to walls along with the most desper-

ate criminals. There, in the presence of the incred-
ulous Jacobin commissioner Georges Couthon
(himself a cripple confined to a wheelchair), Pinel
proposed striking off the fetters that bound the
moaning bundles of skin and bones. His hands
working hard on his chair, Couthon wheeled himself from the scene, and Pinel passed among the
demented like an apostle armed with a holy power,
freeing them from their shackles. Some of them
hung on his coat and trousers like abject animals,
crying with adoration and hatred.

Was this not admirable, Michel Foucault? Parkman, at any rate, supposed so. That Pinel had since
devoted his life to the principle of the curability of
the insane, of their potential rehabilitation into
useful society, seemed to him a noble use of days.
That Pinel's regime among the men of Bicêtre and
the women of Salpêtrière (curious, he noted, how
disproportionately more women lunatics there
seemed to be) was one of the management of
conduct by rewards and punishments, he thought
wholly appropriate. It was inevitable that a superintendent of such houses, if he were to be at all
effective, should be a stern father and judge of the
patients if he were truly to be their friend. Parkman enrolled himself with Pinel and his anointed
deputy, Esquirol, and walked with them through
the long wards, seeing that the food was nutritious
(and not gastro-neurologically disturbing); that the
air was as salubrious as might be compatible with a

Parisian existence; that those who broke into spasms of violent raving could be restrained without excessive brutality. He was attentive; he marked things in his notebook: the classifications of the insane (*manie; démence; frénésie*), how some lost souls would refuse all sustenance, how others would find any clothing insupportable. He attempted to investigate what in their earlier lives might have led to their mental dissolution, for it was an article of faith among the doctors that the sickness required a disorderly life in which to propagate its power.

Most of all, Parkman dreamed of establishing such an asylum in Boston. It would differ from Pinel's establishments in one important respect. Borrowing from the Yorkshireman Tuke's belief in the therapy of nature, he would build a house somewhere beyond the city, on a pleasant hill, surrounded by oaks and beeches. He imagined a place much like a gentleman's villa: with a pedimented door, Ionic columns (or at least pilasters) and sash windows; full of light and fresh air. Outside, patients would busy themselves by raising green vegetables, milking cows or gathering honey from the hospital hives. All of this would be administered, as Dr. Rush had recommended, in a spirit of "mildness, patience, forbearance and encouragement"—though with a strong enough dose of Pinelian firmness to contain disruption. In time, many such victims, now wandering in unreason, would be made reasonable again; those who had lost their true nature would find it.

Before returning to America to begin this work, George Parkman toured Europe to compare other institutions with what he had seen in Paris. He journeyed to the French provinces, to Bordeaux, Avignon, Marseille and then on to Italy. In Rome he avoided the *Apollo Belvedere* and other specimens of the ideal torso in favour of stricken bodies lying in the *ospedale* where, he commented, "the Surgeons, as I have seen them in other parts of Italy, were very shabby looking gentry. In their treatment of ulcers the unfailing routine is to pull off the last dressing and clap on a fresh one, *voilà tout.*" In Florence he sought out Galileo's telescope rather than Donatello's *David,* and in the military hospital moved among beds full of youths whose brilliant uniforms and Napoleonic delusions had been shredded under fire. In one bed lay a twenty-one-year-old who, Parkman wrote to Dr. Warren, "had lost his reason at the moment he was drawn for the army and has been silent, sad and stupid ever since."

Then in Pisa he beheld a great marvel: a human skin peeled away entirely from the body, the subcutaneous blood vessels stained to reveal their capillary tracks. Parkman followed the process of unpeeling with astonishment. That the human casing could, with a snip here and a cut there, a tug here and a pull there, be so perfectly removed seemed to him a miracle of delicacy and cohesion. Once dislodged intact, its oil was wiped clean and the whole dermis hung up to be air-dried. What remained was a garment of translucent parchment that turned creamy yellow-white, mapped with the tracing of the blood paths beneath. It was an empty person, exquisitely designed. If only the filling could be made to match the packing, how truly godlike might be the result!

In 1813 he returned to America via London, where in Bedlam he saw lunatics who had killed chained to the floor for the rest of their lives. This would not do. Back in Boston Parkman burned to translate Pinel's principles and practices into a Massachusetts asylum, an institution of humanity and right reason. He had no doubt that such a place was needed, for he had circulated among clergy-men, physicians and even postmasters throughout the state inquiring about the exact numbers of the insane receiving or needing seclusion and treat-ment. As a first step, he opened a small house in the city where his working methods could be applied, but his sights were set on something much gran-der, the first Massachusetts asylum.

As luck would have it, the Massachusetts Gen-eral Hospital (installed in one of Charles Bulfinch's most elegantly classical pavilions) was contemplat-ing the very same possibility. Parkman the phy-sician and Parkman the property broker came together to promote the project. His unconcealed desire to be the superintendent was supported by two publications, the first a tract called *Remarks on Insanity,* in which the sickness was defined as "want of control of our feelings and propensities" and the Pinelian categories of delirium, melancholy, hypochondria, dementia and idiocy were set out. Each needed its own care and each (even idiocy) had its own possibilities of cure. In his pamphlet *The Management of Lunatics,* Parkman imagined an asylum that would "seldom be viewed as an object of terror"; one where inmates would be received "with the courtesy due a stranger" but be carefully kept from anything that might intensify their distress. This might include other persons, especially those of the opposite sex. (Above all, Pinel had taught Parkman, the patients had to be watched.) Their diet should include items that stimulated the appetite—sausages, anchovies, oysters, smoked beef, ham and salmon—but should some succumb to the urge to fast (as many did) they should not be forced to feed but gradually enticed into sustenance.

Obstinate failure to empty the bladder or bowels at healthy intervals demanded more serious intervention. Laxatives and emetics would be supplied. And since physical conditions as much as moral dispositions were the first necessities for a cure, Parkman imagined a warm bath in which the patient would be enclosed beneath a wooden cover as a stream of cold water was dripped onto his head.

Parkman failed to secure the appointment. It was his money, he thought, not his medicine, that had conspired against him, or rather what the Hospital thought he had offered *to do* with his money. He had discovered and acquired in Roxbury, a mile south of Boston, a mansion formerly belonging to the British Governor Shirley and ideally placed for an asylum of the semi-rustic kind he envisaged. Inmates would be gradually coaxed back to their senses while contemplating river banks. To secure the house, he had put up a portion of the sixteen-thousand-dollar price. He now offered to raise the balance (from among his wide circle of friends and well-wishers). The Hospital committee mistook him to mean he would complete the purchase and indeed endow the building from his own resources.

George Parkman hated misunderstandings of this kind. He responded first with awkwardness, then with vexation, then with embarrassment. He saw himself (not unreasonably) as the man of honour in the business. Could not the trustees see it might appear that he had bought his way into the position? All they did see, however, was bad faith and unfortunate entanglement with an eccentric and mercurial man; not the best person to manage such a new and delicate enterprise. Instead, Rufus Wyman, a disciple of the Yorkshire doctor Tuke and much favoured by the powerful Holyoke, was appointed as the first superintendent of McLean.

It was a hard thing, being spurned in such a

manner. All the expectations that had distinguished him from being a mere creature of his birth, place and property had now been stripped from him. It was especially hard because some money matter had come between him and his vocation. Physicians, after all, were practical men, often, indeed, men of business who seldom hesitated to offer their reputations in the market-place in return for a handsome understanding. Open a Boston newspaper and one could see the most eminent men, the very President of Amherst College, Professor Hitchcock, endorse Ayers Cherry Pectoral, professing himself to be "satisfied that it is an admirable compound for the relief of laryngial and bronchial difficulties," or Boston's most famous surgeon, Henry Jacob Bigelow, recommend Dr. Egipsier's patent Irrigator or Self-Acting Enema Fountain. Indeed, it was not that the trustees of the McLean Asylum had been squeamish about the matter of money but perhaps that Parkman had not been acute enough at sounding them on their price.

So the disappointed George Parkman relapsed into his dynastically allotted role of a Man of Property. When his father, Samuel, died in 1835 and left a great pompous space vacant in the mansion at Bowdoin Square, George became the manager of the family estate. Almost as if he sought compensation for his never-forgotten indignity, he proceeded to buy up large tracts of Boston, from the tenements of the South Cove to the wharf streets of the North End to the tree-shaded sidewalks and churches of the West End. The Parkmans would not be effaced from the city's future. There would be a Parkman Chair of Divinity at Harvard and a Parkman Chair of Anatomy at the Medical College, the new building for which would be constructed on land sold, not donated, by George Parkman. The new jail in Charles Street would be a Parkman property, and the United States Court-house would be located in a Parkman house.

Not that he forgot about the unfortunate crazed creatures who had touched his sensibilities so in the long wards of the Paris hospitals. He wrote about them in the *Boston Medical and Surgical Journal* which, together with the *Medical Intelligencer*, he put out from a small press in a back room of his house. He remained then an Authority, and now and again was called on to testify in court whether a prisoner had committed some act of violence while in a fit of insanity. This was only right and proper because so much of his own writing had been concerned with detection as well as rehabilitation. It had been proved, had it not, that certain moral weaknesses or imperfections could very easily lead first to impulsion, then to irrationality and finally to mental havoc. Such dire endings could have banal beginnings: a financial failure; the inability of a woman to secure a spouse (for women, he recalled from Salpêtrière, were especially susceptible). He had himself listed the danger signs: "impatience, petulance, irresponsibility, rashness, avarice, pride, extravagance, dishonesty, political and professional enthusiasm, gourmandizing, venereal diseases, intemperance." Of especial concern was what Dr. Pinel had called *monomanie:* the hidden growth of some terrible and malignant impulse behind a mask of absolute normality, swelling irresistibly until the day it would erupt in an act which the host was quite incapable of mastering.

What would such a person look like? A bank clerk? A preacher? A doctor? A professor of Harvard College?

The bitterness receded. Boston came to know two George Parkmans. There was, to be sure, the exacting landlord, the omnipresent walking rent-collector. But there was also the Parkman who offered his own house as a hospice during epidemics of smallpox, cholera and scarlet fever. He was often to be seen at McLean Asylum in Somerville involved in some project to ease the lot of its inmates. He had already supplied a piano for the patients and in the fall of 1849 had an organ specially made for the hospital chapel. The poetry and pathos of insanity had begun to affect him. He took to writing on William Cowper, who had been caught between succouring evangelism and raving despair. He was especially fond of the steady rhythms of the *Olney Hymns:*

*The Lord will happiness divine*
*On contrite hearts bestow.*
*Then tell me, gracious God, is mine*
*A contrite heart or no?*

Such men as Cowper suffered, he knew, and he was angry with anyone claiming that the insane were ("mercifully," the usual word) devoid of an ability to feel. He remembered a poor demented man in his care "who became stupid and apparently indifferent to everything, extremely filthy" but whose first words after weeks of silence were "Did you know anyone *half* so wretched as I?" After all, Parkman thought, "do dreaming men or unjustly angry, anxious, distressed, envious, suspicious, prejudiced, impatient, petulant, avaricious, proud, enthusiastic, jealous, irresolute [men] suffer less because their feelings result from delusion?"

At about two o'clock in the afternoon of November 23, Dr. Parkman went into the Medical College for his appointment with Professor Webster.

*His purposes will ripen fast*
*Unfolding ev'ry hour*
*The bud may have a bitter taste*
*But sweet will be the flow'r.*

It was something, yes, but was it enough? Was all that might be done, being done? Robert Gould

# SPECIAL
# NOTICE!

## GEO. PARKMAN, M. D.,

**A well known, and highly respect-**ed citizen of BOSTON, left his House in WALNUT STREET, to meet an engagement of business, on Friday last, November 23d, between 12 and 1 o'clock, P. M., and was seen in the Southerly part of the City, in and near Washington Street, in conversation with some persons, at about 5 o'clock of the afternoon, of the same day.

**Any person who can give** infor-mation relative to him, that may lead to his discovery, is earnestly requested to communicate the same immediately to the City Marshall, for which he shall be liberally rewarded.

*BOSTON, Nov. 25th, 1849.*

From the Congress Printing House, (Farwell & Co.) 32 Congress St.

Shaw* felt all of his seventy-two years that morning; uneasy and leaden. This family had suffered enough, had it not, what with Sam, Francis's boy, barely cold in his grave, George's daughter, Harriette, so sickly and unlikely ever to be well and now her father. Well, it didn't do moping about it. What was being done? That was the issue now.

Patrick, George's Irish servant, his *only* servant, had called earlier in the morning, stammering and fretful. When Shaw had finally got him to speak up, it seemed that his master had not been home all night and his mistress was afeard what could have happened. *Not home all night?* Why, he had never known his brother-in-law to miss his two o'clock dinner, much less wander off without notice. He was the most punctual man he ever knew; even over-punctual to the point of oddness, he would say. So what could have come between the Doctor and his table?

Overnight, he noticed as the carriage climbed Beacon Hill, the weather had turned sharply colder. In Walnut Street he had found Elizabeth Parkman distraught, uncomprehending, tearful. He had done his best to calm her, but her composure dissolved when Patrick brought in a brown paper bag. Inside was a lettuce, looking the worse

*Robert Gould Shaw (1776–1853) was the grandfather of Robert Gould Shaw (1837–1863) who was colonel of the Fifty-Fourth Massachusetts Regiment and died leading his black troops in an attack on Fort Wagner.

for wear. The Doctor had left it at Paul Holland's store, Patrick said, and Mrs. Parkman knew straight away he had got it for his invalid daughter. Always a great believer in the power of diet was the Doctor.

A visit to brother Francis did little to allay anyone's fears. George was, he reminded them, a little queer in his ways. The world saw him as rock-steady, but the family knew him as mercurial. With all that lingering interest in the deranged, was it not possible he had himself wandered off while not quite in full possession of his faculties? Shaw drummed his fingers irritably on a table. He could scarcely credit such a thing; why only yesterday morning George had been his usual bustling, opinionated self, with not a trace of depression. He stared meaningfully at his habitually melancholy brother-in-law.

At nephew Blake's, in Court Street, more grimly practical reasons for the disappearance readily suggested themselves. George was known to be in the habit of carrying large sums of money, rent he had collected, on his person. He might have fallen victim to the kind of reckless crime that had lately inundated Boston. Or perhaps there had been malice aforethought. There was a fellow who had been punished for stealing from the Doctor's house. Might he not have harboured a grudge?

A call to the felon's attorney, though, suggested the man had been out of the city for some while.

Stumbling about for explanations, Blake and Shaw finally called on Marshal Tukey. He neither ventured an opinion on what might have happened nor did they press him for one. Instead, he offered a series of measures, carefully graduated in their seriousness. An advertisement should be placed in the papers, and his men would begin to try and trace Dr. Parkman's movements. But all such reports came to a dead halt before the West Boston Iron Foundry shortly before two. By the afternoon, the more earnest program was executed. Assuming the worst, the Marshal sent men out in lighters to drag the Charles River; even to dive into its viscous green soup for a sight of anything ominous. Nothing. Toll-house keepers on the bridges and turn-pikes were interrogated, especially after one had told Dr. Parkman's agent, Kingsley, that he thought he had seen him bloodied and bent in a carriage driving to Cambridge.

A new notice, dictated by Shaw, was printed up as a handbill, in twenty-eight thousand copies, giving exact details of Parkman's dress that day (purple vest, black stock) and rather less precise details of his remarkable physiognomy. The second paragraph put together the several forebodings of the family.

Three thousand dollars! It was a great deal, Shaw knew, but what of it? What was all his estate—the ships and the bank and the commission houses and the properties—what was it all

# $3,000
# REWARD!

## DR. GEORGE PARKMAN,

**A well known citizen of Boston, left his residence**
No. 8 Walnut Street, on Friday last, he is 60 years of age ;—about 5 feet 9 inches high—grey hair—thin face— with a scar under his chin—light complexion—and usually walks very fast. He was dressed in a dark frock coat, dark pantaloons, purple silk vest, with dark figured black stock and black hat.

As he may have wandered from home in consequence of some sudden aberration of mind, being perfectly well when he left his house; or, as he had with him a large sum of money, he may have been foully dealt with. The above reward will be paid for information which will lead to his discovery if alive; or for the detection and conviction of the perpetrators if any injury may have been done to him. A suitable reward will be paid for the discovery of his body.

*Boston, Nov. 26th, 1849.*       **ROBERT G. SHAW.**
Information may be given to the City Marshal.

worth against the lives of his family? His good-looking bony features settled themselves again into a weary frown. Was enough being done? Had he to do it all himself? What, God forbid, would he do without George, crazy as he was? Should he ever see him again in the flesh, or would he have to listen to him, indeterminate in form and voice, at one of his Spiritualist seances? He shivered at the thought and sunk into an armchair, exhausted.

In the pews of Boston the following morning, in Baptist temples, Congregationalist chapels or Unitarian churches, there was much whispering behind gloved hands, meaningful exchanges of glances and eye-rolling, not always guided by the Spirit. In the pulpit of the New Church in Hanover Street (where George had many tenants among the idolatrous Papists), Francis Parkman's place was taken by a fellow pastor. He had to stay with the family, to try to offer some comfort to Elizabeth and Harriet, especially since young George was still away in Germany.

They got through the day as best they could, polite speech and turbulent emotion separated by a great black distance. At about four, a caller was announced. It was Professor John Webster, everyone's friend.

# 3

# Enterprise: The Janitor

*Friday, November 30, 1849*

"Well, Ephraim," said Marshal Tukey to the janitor, "and was it the turkey Mr. Webster gave you 'that made you so suspicious'?"

"I should say not, Sir," he replied, not meeting the Marshal's steady gaze. "It were well before that, on Sunday, that I thought I should watch the Professor, and I told the wife I'd do it, even though she was none too happy about such a snooping and a prying."

"But the turkey, Ephraim," the Marshal insisted with a kind of serious merriment not appropriate to the moment, "did you eat it, then, you and Mrs. Littlefield?"

"Wouldn't it have been a sin to waste it, with us making the holiday on the pretty little the College pays us?"

"And was it a good bird, the Professor's turkey?"

"Good enough." The janitor had always been uneasy in the presence of the Marshal. Tukey had a way of looking hard and direct at you out of those grey eyes so you didn't know what he was up to.

"So on Thanksgiving you had your dinner and then set to work to find the body?"

"I were mighty tired of all the talk, wherever I went, in the market and the Lodge, as to how if they were to find the Doctor it would be in the Medical College, and all those queer looks coming my way as if I had something to do with the business. I reckoned seeing as how your men had been through the place, all that was left was the privy vault, and if nothing was there, that would be the end of it."

"But you thought there might be something there, didn't you, Ephraim?"

"I don't know what I thought, Sir, I wanted to be done with it, I know that."

"And the reward, Mr. Littlefield," Tukey asked, shifting to a less familiar form of address, "assuming that what we have are the remains of the Doctor, will you be collecting Mr. Shaw's money?"

"Have I ever said I would, Mr. Tukey?" the janitor replied, with a note of anger sharpening the edge of his low voice, yet not quite answering the question.

He lifted his face at last to meet the policeman's and stared back. A long moment of embarrassed silence followed. Why, with all that had happened this day and him still a-trembling with it all, was he the one to get such questions as these? Why should

Portrait of Ephraim Littlefield.

it be he who had to explain himself? He was more deserving of commendations, surely; he asked for nothing more.

Littlefield looked round at the other men, three of them sitting on his best green chairs in his little parlour. Mr. Shaw's old face looked white and stricken by what he had seen. The younger Dr. Bigelow, the surgeon, had his chin cupped in his hands and was looking desolate. Bigelow had been rough enough with him when Littlefield had run into the Doctor's house with the dirt and gashes of his work still on him; Bigelow had shaken him, called him crazy and such names. He was quiet enough now, wasn't he? The two other policemen were more themselves. Derastus Clapp, the detective, had his little leather book out and was scribbling something, while Constable Trenholm was standing by the door as though expecting intruders.

The Marshal got up quite abruptly, as though he were addressing a public meeting: "Well, gentlemen, I suppose we know what must be done. Secure an order for the Professor's arrest, Mr. Clapp; find him and bring him here. He shall see this and we shall see how he conducts himself."

Everyone but the janitor and Trenholm departed—the detective to Cambridge to seek the Professor; Shaw and Bigelow to their houses on Summer and Chauncy Streets. The Marshal walked slowly back to his office, trying to clear his head in the sharp night air. He should not have badgered Littlefield, but the truth was he minded the janitor having done so much and his own officers so little.

He minded still more his own disbelief earlier in the week when the janitor had come to him with his suspicions. Damn him and damn Webster; what business had a Harvard Professor and Cambridge gentleman committing murder. Hadn't he enough on his hands with the city a stagnant pond: scum on the top and the scuttling of reptiles down below? The politicians were on his back again, and every time Wendell Phillips opened his singsong mouth on the Common about Free-Soil and the slaves, people's heads got broken. Mayor Quincy was his friend alright but there would be a new mayor, a Bigelow, next year and he was not to be counted on.

What did they want of him, these gentlemen? He had come to them out of the Maine woods, a mechanic's son but nobody's gull. Two years at the Law School in Cambridge had taught him more than the law: how the brethren of the profession comported themselves and how they set a polite distance between themselves and his kind. But they needed him all the same. And he had given them what they wanted: arrests; a great many arrests, of whores and thieves and drunks and tavern-keepers without licences and, yes, dog-keepers without licences. This very year he had caught the city's most famous burglar, "Bristol Bill" Warberton, a damn clever scoundrel. He and Clapp had even got the property back for them. Whenever he felt put upon he brought to mind the sweet memory of his men digging straight into the Common for the stolen money, and the crowds gathering and the politicians coming from the State-house to see. When the box was hauled up, there was never such a cheering; he still had to smile at the thought of it. They had their little satisfactions though, the "First Men," bringing him up before the magistrate for fast driving over and again. Didn't they understand how he, Francis Tukey, should be seen: in black horse and carriage flying through the city for their law, their order?

And this sorry business; what good would it do him or his men? Why should it make him so out of sorts? The remains had been vilely dealt with, but he had seen worse. No, it was the humbug that made him feel sick; the straight-faced, sober-sided, lily-livered gentlemen who protested so much when he brought carts full of villains for their due, who told him what was and what wasn't right; the humbug was so beguiling he sometimes started to feel it coming on himself. He knew he cut a figure in this town: big, curly haired, the handsome *bhoy* with a revolver in his coat. He had power; he could scare people alright. What he wanted now was grace, some decent courtesy from those moneyed weaklings whose persons and property he guarded. Ah, what was there to it, all this high holiness, but the rotten smell of faded flowers in dirty water?

In the parlour, Ephraim Littlefield sat nursing an unformed sense of grievance.

They made their mark, all those niggling questions from the Marshal. You would think, wouldn't you, after all I'd done, that the Marshal might be more accommodating? Hadn't I saved them from foolishness; hadn't I known what was coming, all along? Just because I was their skivvy don't mean I don't have a head on my shoulders. You learn a lot tending their stoves, washing their sinks, clearing their trash and generally cleaning up after the Professors; not just what they did but what they were. They all thought themselves such gentlemen, but some were and some weren't. Mr. Holmes now and Mr. Jackson, they were the salt of the earth and could say good morning without making it sound like an order, and old Dr. Bigelow, who could say a word against him, unlike that son of his with his stuck-up airs and his French cabriolet?

As for Webster, there had always been bad feeling between us, ever since I started as janitor seven years ago. Then in 1846 when the new College had

been built on Dr. Parkman's land, I found myself
sharing the lower floor with Dr. Webster's laboratory; we got on no better, a good deal worse really.
He had always been at me like some yapping dog:
Littlefield did you leave the windows open again;
Littlefield have you been playing cards in my room
again? Well, he never found me at it did he? And
what if I had, what harm was there in that, a few
fellows for company and no damage done to person or property? I knew as how Webster wanted to
be rid of me, years ago, and how he had told stories
to the Dean, but nothing could come of it, could it.
And now who was the villain, eh?

Well, I have done some bad things in my time,
like many men, but nothing so bad as this. I never
liked it, having to sell cadavers to the students for
dissection at twenty-five dollars a body, but how
was I and Caroline and the children to live on the
pittance the College paid me otherwise? In the
taverns they called me a "resurrection man" and
said that I had dug up fresh graves on the Common
and on Copp's Hill to supply the students, but it
was all stories, mostly; only I didn't ask questions of
those who gave him the bodies. These days, with
all them dying of the cholera and in a filthy state,
there was a premium on a clean, fresh corpse, so I
was doing everyone a good service wasn't I, being
the middleman? The one time I had gone out in
the night to do it myself I gagged from the badness
of it and the smell of mushrooms from the earth,

and threw up into the grave and swore off ever doing it again.

Now Dr. Parkman, in his queer way, he would understand what a man had to do for his living. Didn't he do some rum things himself for the extra penny? And he knew the value of the dollar, by God. So when he started showing up at Webster's lectures, standing at the back of the wall, waiting for him to finish, it had to be some business with money. Then ten days or so ago, the two of them had a pretty sharp exchange, the Doctor just sailing into the Professor's back room while Webster was reading his chemistry book with a candle. The intrusion itself got him steamed up, but it got worse when the Doctor fairly shouted at him, "Are you ready for me tonight?" or some such. Then there was a fair to-do right under my nose, the Doctor with his high voice talking about some mortgage on goods already spoken for and getting red in the face and waving papers at the Professor, and him going white and trying to keep calm and myself trying to keep out of it but hear it all at the same time. "Doctor, something must be accomplished to-morrow," Parkman said to Webster before he left in that hurried way of his, but I never saw him come back the next day.

Then a day or so afterwards, Professor Webster had asked all those questions about the dissecting-room vault—the hole where the trash from the cadavers was slung. There had been men down there fixing a leak in the wall next to the coal pen so that the smell didn't get over the building, and now it was covered with earth and dirt to seal it up. Why should he be so interested in that vault and the way down to it, and whether a lantern could be kept lit down there? I told him I had had trouble doing that when I went to fetch an African skull Mr. Ainsworth wanted to macerate, and then there was a silence till he said as how he needed some gas for one of his chemistry experiments and the vapours in the vault would be just the thing.

I hadn't put anything much together then, hadn't seen any connexions you could say were peculiar, even after I heard the news of Dr. Parkman's disappearance. On the Sunday when the first handbills were plastered up, I had gone out with a whole gang of people to search around some of the neighbourhood and look into some of the Doctor's tenements to see if some foul play had been done to him. That afternoon as the sun was setting, Webster had come up to me by the College and asked me if I had seen Dr. Parkman on the Friday, and I had said, yes, just before dinner time that afternoon coming towards the College door. It was then that the Professor had struck his cane, a heavy polished thing with some sort of silver knob on it, hard on the sidewalk, so hard he might have cracked it. It was so sudden and so violent I started a bit, and then he went on to tell me as how it was at that very time that he had seen the Doctor in his room and had paid him $483 and some cents owing to him. The Doctor, he said, took it, struck a line through the mortgage paper and dashed off saying he would have it discharged at the Cambridge office.

I wondered at all this information, me not having asked it and out it comes just the same and in such detail too, the exact number of dollars and even of cents as if he was a book-keeper. And all the time he said this, he kept his head down not at all like he usually did. Usually he'd look at me direct, through those specs of his, as though he meant something harder in between the words. But it was the crack of that cane of his that I heard over and again that night; how he didn't hit it true; how the force of it was too much and sideways against the flagstone. Then everything seemed to fall into place: how I'd seen Dr. Webster coming down the stairs with a candle Friday afternoon at five o'clock or thereabouts, much later than ever he did, and how when I'd gone in to sweep up his rooms on Saturday like I always did, I found the doors bolted from the inside.

I woke Caroline and told her right out I thought he'd done something to the Doctor and how as I was going to keep a look-out on everything he did.

"Oh Eph," says she, "I'm afraid you don't know what you're doing; and suppose it ain't so and even suppose it is so, do you think the professors would believe one of their kind could do such a thing?"

"I don't know what they'll believe," I says, "but all I know is I saw the Doctor on his way here and how the other week he had said hard words to Webster about finishing things and that since then things have happened here that haven't happened before and I mean to find out why."

I had to do most of it myself, didn't I, since the police were so dull about it. Why, on the Monday when the officer, Mr. Starkweather, came with Mr. Kingsley, the Doctor's agent, to look round the College, they seemed to tiptoe around as though it was a waste of time. And this when Dr. Webster's rooms were still bolted fast. When he opened up to my knocking, I showed them how the rooms were arranged, the little laboratory and the private study at the back of his lecture room, with a stair leading from that room down to the lower laboratory. They went down and looked about the dissecting room and the lab, I suppose, but they didn't take much time about it.

Even on Tuesday morning when Mr. Clapp came with two other officers, Mr. Rice and Mr. Fuller, I wasn't sure they meant business. They gave us some story about wanting to search all the houses in the neighbourhood and getting entry better if they could say they had looked over the College first. Perhaps it changed when the Professor wouldn't come to his door until after I had banged on it with knuckles and then with fists and then given it a fine pounding as hard as I could.

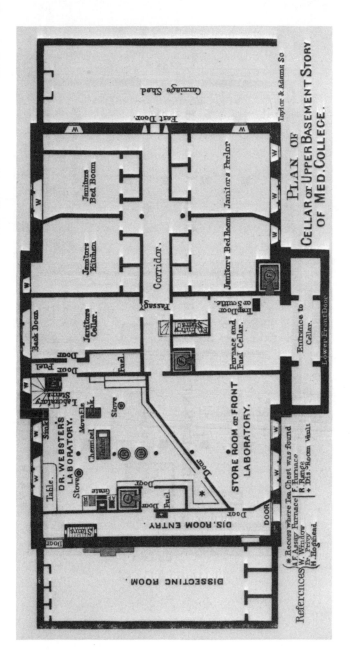

PLAN OF CELLAR or UPPER BASEMENT STORY OF MED. COLLEGE.

Taylor & Adams Sq

Carriage Shed

East Door.

Janitors Bed Room

Janitors Kitchen

Back Room

Janitors Cellar.

Corridor.

Passage

Janitor's Bed Room

Janitor's Parlor

Trap Door or Scuttle.

Furnace and Fuel Cellar.

Entrance to Cellar.

Lower Front Door

W. Privy

Fuel

Door

Door Fuel

Laboratory Stairs

Smoke

DR. WEBSTER'S LABORATORY.

Table.

Laboratory Store

Chemical Store

Movable

Store

Grate

Store

Door

Door

Fuel

STORE ROOM or FRONT LABORATORY.

Door

DOOR

DIS. ROOM ENTRY.

Stairs

Door

Stairs

DISSECTING ROOM.

References
{
* Recess where Tea Chest was found
A. F. Assay Furnace  F. Furnace
W. Window  R. Range
Pr. Privy  + Dis. Room Vault
H. Hogshead
}

MASS. MEDICAL COLLEGE

Standing there in that queer cap of his and the blue
overalls, he seemed a lot more jittery than the day
before, and warned Mr. Clapp to look out for what
he called his dangerous things in his back room:
powders and glass vessels and minerals and such.
It's true some of the lads had done some mischief
to precious minerals some time back and he got
fair worked up then, but he seemed more excited
about it all than his science allowed for.

It was even more fishy, I thought, when we went
downstairs to the lower laboratory. Mr. Clapp
asked about Webster's own privy, and right away
the doctor went to unbolt a door to one of the
store-rooms to turn their attention away from it.

The dissecting-room vault was staring us all in

the face, of course. Later on they told me it was too obvious a place to make it likely anything would be put there, and at the time, since I had the lock and key to it and had seen nothing just a while back, I didn't give it much thought myself. Still, we peered inside it and saw nothing and even went down the little trap-door right under the building into the little crawl space. That just left the Professor's privy to see to. He alone had the key to it, so I told them how the only way into it would be to knock a hole in from the underside and none of them volunteered, so we left it at that.

It was that same afternoon that his manner altered, became, I don't know, slacker, for he unbolted some of the doors at last. When I saw him in his back room, he asked me if we had our turkey yet and when I said I thought we might eat out this year on Thanksgiving, he went right ahead anyway and made me the gift of one from Mr. Foster's next to the Howard Athenaeum. He said he might want an odd job or two done, I suppose in return, but it still didn't make it less peculiar, him never having given me so much as ten cents before.

Next morning, the Wednesday, I could hear him moving about downstairs and felt so vexed at not seeing what he was up to I tried peering through the keyhole of the store-room door; then I chipped out with my knife a piece big enough to let me see in. I think I must have made a cracking noise for he suddenly stopped walking about. I laid myself full-stretch on the floor and got a squinny beneath the door, enough to see him coming and going with the coal hod and bundles of wood. The wife came out and saw me then and got flustered and told me to come away then and there, and since we had to do our marketing, I did as she told me.

All that morning, though, my mind was far away from sweet potatoes and harvest corn. I was of a mind to do more and see more, but I was still taken by surprise, when I got back, to feel the wall near the laboratory was hot. I supposed it could only be the little furnace that was never used and determined somehow to see if it was truly alight. With all the doors still locked and bolted, the only way was to climb up my cellar wall and through one of his laboratory windows. Just fancy—what with him always telling me to shut the windows—he had left one unfastened himself. Once in, I couldn't see much fire, but a big part of the barrels kindling was gone along with a good part of the water in one of the hogsheads.

So I knew what had to be done, didn't I? It were a shame, I guess, that it was the holiday to do it, but I reckoned at least the Professor would be at home and I could get on with it undisturbed. We had our dinner on his turkey, the children pitching in with a will. Then in the afternoon I dropped down through the trap with a lantern, a hatchet and a mortise-chisel. It was hard to keep the lantern alight down there, and the space was about four feet high, so I was bent double, my knees on the slimy dirt. In an hour and a half all I could do was to batter through a couple of layers of the brick beneath the privy, all the while choking on the dust and scraping my wrists and knuckles against the stone. At times I thought it were hopeless; that I was a crazy person doing a reckless thing, and at times I was scared that there would be nothing and I should be found out and Webster would have his wish and get me dismissed the way he had long wanted and at times I imagined some formless thing, a rank jelly, might wash in from the Charles and cover me.

I wasn't going on at night, for sure, and climbed out of it in time to take Caroline to the Sons of Temperance Ball as I had promised. There we buttoned our lips and forgot for a while what a state we were in. I danced eighteen of the numbers on the card, not all with the wife. I like my dances and think I cut a good enough figure a-strutting and a-twirling.

That was but yesterday, but it seems an age. We didn't get back till four in the morning, but it was no time to be slumbering, so I was up at nine when Dr. Webster actually came in to see us in the kitchen. He took the paper from the table and asked if there were any more news of Dr. Parkman. He told us that in the apothecary's they had a tale of a woman who had seen a big bundle put in a cab and when they had found the cab (from its number), it was discovered to be bloody inside. "There are so many flying reports about I am sure I don't know what to believe," he said.

I wanted to carry on with the work, but couldn't take the loneliness of it any more, so I went to Dr. Henry Bigelow and then to Dr. Jackson and told them what I was up to. It was a hard thing because I didn't know if they mightn't bawl me out or forbid me going on with it. But they both said I should persevere, Dr. Jackson saying, "Mr. Littlefield, I feel dreadfully about this; and do you go through that wall before you sleep tonight." He is a good man, and I am sure he hoped nothing would come of it for all our sakes and the sake of the College. If I was to find anything, I said I'd go straight to Dean Holmes, but he said, no, I should go instead to old Dr. Jacob Bigelow.

I knew I needed stronger tools and borrowed myself a crowbar from Fullers around the corner, telling Leonard some story about setting a pipe in through a brick wall. "I guess you do," he came back, looking at me in a funny kind of way. When I got back to the College, I dropped the deadbolt on the front door so as to forestall Dr. Webster and told the wife to give four raps if he were to approach. Poor thing, she had no stomach to be a look-out but had given up trying to warn me off the work especially now she knew two of the Professors had given their blessing to the enterprise.

I wasn't long down there before I knew I'd need

something still stronger than the crowbar if I was to get through, what with my hands all bloody and blistered already. I got some gloves and a hammer and a big chisel from the Fullers and banged away till all of a sudden I heard Caroline's four knocks and got up out of the space as quick as possible. But it was only Mr. Kingsley and Mr. Starkweather and Caroline half smiling, half upset at her mistake. I couldn't somehow say anything to them what I was at. A few minutes later, I saw Mr. Trenholm, and though he were police too, since I knew him better around the neighbourhood beat I told him and said I might be through the wall in half an hour or so. Then the wife came in and said, "You've just saved your bacon as Dr. Webster has passed in." He came up to Mr. Trenholm and me and mentioned the Irishman who'd paid for a one cent toll with a twenty dollar bill and how suspicious the Marshal thought that was.

Twenty minutes or so later when I was sure he had gone for the day, I went back down. It was getting dark, not that it made any difference down in that rat-hole, but I felt the cold even as I was sweating through the labour. I knew there couldn't be much left, yet as the sound of the hammer knocking against the brick suddenly changed I became afraid again and stopped what I was doing, wiped the dirt away from my eyes with my bloody, blistered hands and just sat on my haunches for a moment to catch my breath. Then I thought of how

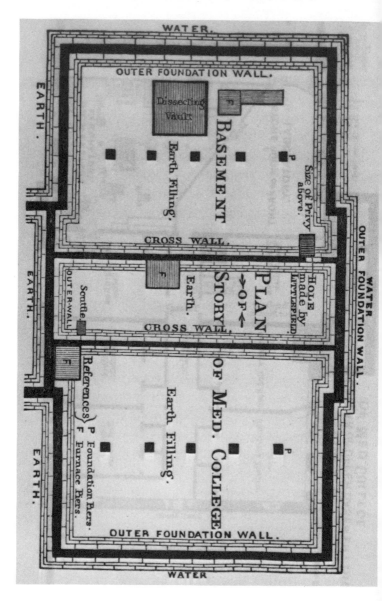

far I had come and what was to be the issue of all this and how there could be no going back whatever the resolution. So I raised myself up against the face of the wall, with my back bent, and gave the mightiest swing with the blunt end of the crowbar and I near as fell forward as I was through. The rush of air from the hole near put out my light and I had to shelter it carefully as I broadened the gap enough to put both the lantern and my face through the opening.

I wanted to scream and cry, and in a way I don't rightly understand, laugh all at once. For there they were sure enough, lying in a pile propped up against a mound of dirt. I knew enough about bodies and bones—hadn't I been carting them about all my life—to recognise what I saw: a pelvis with the doings all hanging down from it, some pieces of leg and the Cochituate water from the sink above running down over them like some fountain. And until that very moment, for all my suspicions growing and building up and up, I still had no idea what I might see, had never pictured to myself how it might look. Perhaps I was expecting a body; perhaps nothing; but not these bits of butcher's trash sitting on the wet dirt. They were so white, you see, so clean and white.

I scrambled back up as fast as I could, meaning to tell Dr. Bigelow right away. But when I saw the wife and she saw me and said, "Why Eph, dear, what's the matter, have you found something?" I couldn't help but busting out crying and bawling as if I were a babe in terror. She sat me down and poured me a drop of brandy we save even though I'm supposed to be a Son of Temperance these days, and I got my composure back some, enough to take myself round to Dr. Jacob Bigelow's in Summer Street. It was only that he wasn't there that made me go to young Dr. Henry Bigelow's in Chauncy Street; and when I was there and told him my story and he started a-yelling at me and telling me I was crazy, I regretted ever having come at all. Still, we went on to Mr. Shaw's, where we found the Marshal.

The Marshal told me to go back to the College, and when I got there, I found George Trenholm had already been down and seen the pieces of body. Soon after, the Marshal and Colonel Clapp and Dr. Bigelow and Mr. Shaw came, and we all went down together in the dirt and dust. I wondered at Mr. Shaw wanting to do this, he being more elderly, and as we crawled the sixty feet I thought he might swoon, but he stayed strong enough to reach the hole. The Marshal put his head in and asked Dr. Bigelow to say if these were human remains or no, and he didn't hesitate. He knew as well as I this was not the right place for anything that might have come from the dissecting room and told the Marshal so. Just then we heard some running and all started at once, the Marshal pulling out his gun and us all saying at once, "It's him, it's him," though when we all got out in a hurry we found it was only the wife and children running around. Caroline won't come out of the kitchen now and talk to us; she has taken all this badly I think and wants neither to hear nor see any more of it.

"Mr. Littlefield," says the Marshal, "this furnace you spoke of. I think we had better take a look at it."

So we walked into the lower laboratory, and Mr. Clapp went straight to the furnace, opened the hatch, reached as far as he could into the ashes, started a little and pulled out a big piece of bone, grey and sooty. I knew straight away what it was. He stood there for a minute, his own arm holding on to the forearm of another. I went to take a look myself, but the Marshal took it from me as if it was a weapon and spoke with uncommon gentleness.

"Come, Mr. Littlefield; this is enough. We had better wait."

We went back to the parlour, and he spoke to me in quite a different tone of turkeys and rewards and such like before he went off leaving me with George Trenholm.

It's getting late now and I'm worn out from all this labour. How will it be when they bring him here to see this; how will he regard me who have been his menial all these years?

It must have been eleven o'clock. Caroline and the children were asleep when the front door-bell rang. On the steps there was a big crowd, police-men and others—I don't know how many. In their midst was Mr. Clapp holding up Dr. Webster, for he looked half-dead and half-crazed, like I had never seen him before. He looked at me once with fear and rage all mixed up in his blinking eyes. But then he got taken upstairs to his rooms and paid me no more attention.

# 4
# Debt: Skyrocket Jack

Skyrocket Jack? Oh, he was affability itself, was
Professor John Webster, a man who lived to make
others cheerful. You could see it in his frame and
deportment, an endomorph: plump and padded,
curly haired, a beaming countenance; expansive
salutations, a warm handshake, an open door, a
thoughtful host, a dab hand at whist (careful to lose
to the ladies), a man with a firm grip on the neck of
the decanter and a constantly inviting expression.
In the cause of conviviality he was resourceful, too.
Was he not the inventor of the Class Day Spread—
a feast of pasties and dainties and summer punch
set out on crisp linen in Harvard Yard? Had he not
insisted on fireworks to mark the inauguration of
handsome President Everett? His was the other
face of Yankeedom; as genial and open as George
Parkman's was austere and closed. Only three years
separated them (in their Harvard classes, more
important than their birth), but while Dr. Parkman
was often taken to be older than his days, John

# TRIAL

OF

## PROFESSOR JOHN W. WEBSTER,

FOR THE

## MURDER

OF

## DOCTOR GEORGE PARKMAN.

REPORTED EXCLUSIVELY FOR THE N. Y. DAILY GLOBE.

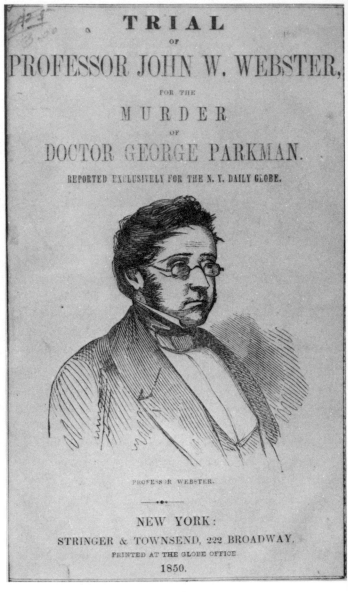

PROFESSOR WEBSTER.

NEW YORK:

STRINGER & TOWNSEND, 222 BROADWAY,

PRINTED AT THE GLOBE OFFICE

1850.

Webster was thought of, by many, as always youthful. Only one voice, and that later too, dissented.
"His phrenology always struck me unfavorably,"
wrote Horace Mann. "I think his head was terribly
wide at the base."

No one, however, doubted John Webster's devotion to his family. Gathered in the domestic nest
were three daughters, invariably referred to in the
sympathetic press as "his three lovely daughters,"
which was no more than fair comment, there being
a fourth lovely daughter married in the Azores. But
three was certainly enough to perform perfectly
delightful musical evenings of piano, flute and
voice for the many guests who came to Cambridge.
There were many such occasions, for the Websters
were well connected by family and profession. The
Professor's mother was a Leverett, another of the
great Harvard dynasties; his wife's sister married
into the Prescotts, among whom young William,
the historian, was losing his sight while pursuing
Cortés and Pizarro along the tracks of their Conquests. The Robert Gould Shaws were friends
enough for them to discuss Spiritualism without
embarrassment; the Reverend Francis Parkman,
Sr., was his Unitarian pastor.

In short, not the kind of man one would in-
stinctively place among the criminal classes. A parade of witnesses would file in and out of the box to
testify that he was a "humane and peaceable man."
President Sparks, who was bold enough to say that

"Harvard professors do not often commit murder," had always thought him "kind and amiable."
Other gentlemen of his acquaintance, prudently
considering the consequences of their testimony,
would avow his *reputation* to be that of a lamb,
while leaving open the possibility that something
else might lie beneath the fleece. He was thought
by the inventor and Rumford Professor Daniel
Treadwell, by the historian Francis Bowen and by
Nathaniel Bowditch inclined to "a quick and irritable temper." He had been upset, even petulant,
when ordered to stop decorating Harvard Hall,
said the painter John Fulton. But if quick to anger,
all were agreed, he would just as quickly forget the
cause of offence. His rocket might flare and fizz
and whistle but would be harmlessly spent.

No, he could not possibly have done such a
thing, thought one of his pupils, James Oliver, for
the Professor had been so timid a fellow. "When I
was in College," the student wrote to the Professor's defence attorney, "it was the regular practice to throw things about Doctor Webster's
lecture room, drop his minerals on the floor till we
fairly pitied him for his meekness. I think I have
seen no other Professor bear so much from his
students. Indeed it was a common story that his
classes had sometimes made him break up the
exercise before the hour and in tears.

"And yet he always told us that he never 'reported' a student to the Faculty because he wished

to get along pleasantly with us! Not every professor can say as much after twenty years' connection with the College.

"I tell you this to show that we did not merely think Dr. Webster a 'peaceable man' but we actually despised his want of spirit and continually imposed on him with impunity."

A sorry spectacle, the Professor put-upon by his students; even sorrier because his ability to set seedcake and Madeira on the table depended on their presence. It was all very fine for the magnates of the Faculty, the Quincys and the Everetts, well-to-do in their own right and made richer by their marriages, to coast along on their stipend. But his pittance—a paltry twelve hundred dollars—could hardly keep the family, much less their social circle, decently entertained. Extra emoluments might be gained from the College if he were to sell a great many tickets to his chemistry lectures. And the opening of the new building in 1846, on Dr. Parkman's land, with its grander spaces, laboratories and dissecting rooms, encouraged him to imagine a new world of instruction: benches crammed with eager, diligent, *respectful,* ticket-paying students.

To his dismay, these throngs failed to materialise. Perhaps he was partly to blame. He could never manage the witty sallies, the elegance of Oliver Wendell Holmes upstairs, from whose rooms there echoed hearty laughter followed by studious silence. Well, at least there were some students alright, and he could overlook their loutish misconduct if their tickets were paid. But somehow there were never enough to make good on his many obligations, let alone for the finer conveniences of life. Such a bitter disappointment for a man who was now in his prime; who had served the College so faithfully; who had such responsibilities, so many unmarried daughters. Grievances chewed at him. Why was the world so unjust? Why had others prospered with so little effort (and so few virtues), whereas he had been singled out for struggle and misfortune?

His adversities seemed all the more cruel when he considered how fair had been his prospects. His pedigree was impeccably Puritan; his grandfather just as much the merchant-prince as old Sam Parkman. He had been born in Anne Street in 1793 before the whores made it their favourite place of commerce, opposite his father's apothecary shop. Removed to Amesbury where the family fortunes had prospered, his father had grown tyrannical with them, keeping him on a niggardly allowance all through his school and college years. Like George Parkman he had studied with the sainted John Warren at the old Medical College on Mason Street and like him he had travelled farther in search of more instruction. London, rather than Paris, became his academy; and instead of the howling corridors of Pinel's asylum, John Webster dwelled among the dark oak walls and red tiles of Guys Hospital. In England he developed the taste for poetry which he passed on to his daughters in their evening reading of Milton and Gray. His name appears on the Guys register directly below that of fellow student John Keats.

He was not, however, completely free of boyish naughtiness. At Harvard the young Webster earned reprimands from the severe gentlemen responsible for keeping discipline over their adolescent charges. In London, so his uncharitable wife's sister Amelia later recollected, there had been talk of a rape, of flight from the country, of another broken betrothal, of another running-away.

Whatever the proximate reasons, in the year that Napoleon was sent to St. Helena, John Webster found himself marooned on the tiny island of São Miguel (St. Michael, as the Anglo-Americans renamed it) in the Azores. Yankees came to the islands for two reasons: whaling and convalescence. Sixty ships from New Bedford and Nantucket put in each year, and the little inns of Ponta Delgada were full of red-faced men drinking their fill before the hunt. But the blue skies, the merry breezes and a little sulphur spring that belched and hissed from a volcanic hillside also made it a station for those seeking therapy for rheumatic joints or wheezing asthmatic lungs. John Webster ministered to both sorts: the swaggering salts and the whey-faced invalids.

Beyond the orange and lemon groves, a little way into the countryside, on a hill dotted with alien plantings of cedar and poplar, lived the American Consul, a Mr. Hickling, with his four daughters. Starved for conversation that turned on neither the current price of spermaceti nor the curative properties of mud, the family made much of the young physician, and before long John Webster—the affable, expansive, educated John Webster—had turned the head of Harriet Hickling. If medicine was his profession, geology was his passion. On walks along the cliffs, or down in extinct craters from whose floor sprouted giant ferns and spongy beds of moss, the bespectacled suitor did his wooing with impressive talk of Cretaceous and Jurassic. He related the primordial heavings and shiftings, eruptions and settlements, oozes and deposits that had produced, at length, Azores rocks. Meaningful pebbles clicked in his palms as he gently lectured his student. Half-listening, Harriet saw a life of grace and dignity, a life at the core of American culture, opening before her. Handsome, modern broughams, nutwood-panelled parlours and the agreeable music of informed conversation seemed to be hers to command. She would be off-island at last, rescued from social shipwreck, given the setting her own qualities surely called for.

In Boston the reality fell sharply short of the dream. Webster went into practice with a Dr.

Gorham but was never quite able to live in the style a gentleman-professional required. As junior partner he seemed to be paying more for equipment and books and the social exercises needed to establish a clientele than he earned. When the apothecary father died, further rude shocks awaited him. The fortune, rumoured to be fifty thousand, was a small fraction of that; much of the capital had been swallowed up in imprudent ventures, had vanished at that indeterminate golden horizon of western speculation; much of the rest subsided with the stock of the Charles River Bridge Company.

As George Parkman withdrew from science to business, John Webster went in the reverse direction. Harvard made him a lecturer in chemistry at the Medical College for eight hundred dollars a year, but what the position wanted in remuneration, Webster felt, it compensated for in distinction, or at least potential distinction. To be, one day, a Harvard Professor, to dwell amidst men of intellect, erudition and lightly worn religion; to be received, *ex officio* as a man of culture; this was surely worth the regrettably thin purse that went with all these blessings. But as time went on and he did indeed become one of the Elect, the Erving Professor of Chemistry, and the eight hundred swelled into all of twelve hundred, his discontents mounted along with his debts.

How could they have been avoided? he asked himself. He could not have asked Harriet and the girls to live in a mean hovel, surely. So the depleted legacy was spent on a swaggering, custom-built house on Concord Street, with a grandiose portico, a fine library and capacious wine cellars. When it burned to the ground in 1866, long after its owner had gone from the scene, it was known to locals as "Webster's Folly."

All this cost dearly. Servants had to be kept. A Professor must needs entertain. Equipping the Medical College was at his own expense, made more expensive because his predecessor in the chair had obliged him to buy the obsolete and ill-used experimental equipment, down to the last cloudy alembic. In addition to which, he needed to satisfy the learned urges that came upon him now and again. He prided himself on building indisputably the best geological cabinet in all of Boston. But seizing opportunities presented to him by workers in the field as well as travelling himself in pursuit of fine specimens meant more expenses.

Then there was the mastodon. A gentleman in New Jersey had let him know a complete skeleton could be his for a mere three thousand dollars! A whole, undivided mastodon! His dreams were haunted by great curving tusks and a noble, pre-historic cranium. How could he refuse? Perhaps Dr. Warren and the College might provide the funds, or at least the major part, for the beast would be housed in the College Museum; would indeed be its triumphant specimen. But Dr. Warren demurred; the College's part was a dwarfish portion; Dr. Webster was already irreversibly committed. He saw the mastodon lumbering away from his reach. Somehow he provided what was called for, and it returned to sit crushingly athwart his shoulders, a mammoth debt.

For ten years John Webster scraped along in such a way, drifting dangerously far from the Bostonian shores of prudent housekeeping, dressing and schooling and dancing his wife and daughters as Cambridge ladies expected to be dressed and schooled and danced. Publications helped supplement the stipend and the sparse lecture tickets. *Webster's Chemistry* became a text-book in American colleges; his translation of the great Justus von Liebig's *Organic Chemistry* joined it on the shelf, along with a definitive mineralogical and geological survey of the Azores.

But it seemed that rocks of the mid-Atlantic would not be enough to spare the Professor painful embarrassment. In 1835, after another speculative disappointment, the Concord Street house had to be sold. Bearing the social disgrace and personal discomfort with commendable fortitude, the Websters removed themselves to Jonas Wyeth's pretty frame house on Garden Street, close to Washington's Elm, where the commander had mustered his men on Cambridge Common. It was certainly not grand but it would do, especially on a long-term lease with an option to buy. If there was no

portico, there were at least pilasters, and an attic
for the servant, who could survey the street from a
sweetly cross-hatched dormer window. There was
a garden, not spacious, but with enough land for
the Professor to transplant hydrangeas and azaleas
that had been carefully shipped from St. Michael
by his sister-in-law.

The retrenchment was not enough. In 1842
creditors became distressingly importunate. But
why else should a man have friends if not to turn to
them in his (temporary) hour of need? He went to
George Parkman, a gentleman famous for his
timely loans, and borrowed four hundred dollars.
Five years later he needed further succour, and a
syndicate of Harvard colleagues and friends—
Prescotts, Bigelows, Cunninghams—rallied round
to come up with another $2,432, the odd fig-
ure incorporating the balance owing to the Doctor. As security for this substantial sum, the
Professor reluctantly put up his most cherished
possession—the collection of geological specimens and minerals. The College had obtusely declined to acquire this from him, notwithstanding
all the pains he had taken to perfect the cabinet.
Very well, it should now be used at least to liberate
him from exigency; for surely his friends would
never call in the collateral.

When the next crisis arrived—for they came
now at shortening intervals—he looked around for
further help. He dimly recalled his father's claims

of a distant relationship to the family of the British Sir Godfrey Webster, who had taken his own life but had left a reputedly vast estate in Maine. Might there be anything in this kinship? he wrote to his friend the historian George Bancroft. Not, of course, that he was imagining anything might be *gained,* any claim on the estate, that is, but was the kinship itself sound? Did Bancroft know anything about the property and its legatees?

With these baronial fantasies evaporating, the Professor had no recourse but to seek help from his friends yet again. He went to see Robert Gould Shaw in Summer Street. A gift was offered. John Webster insisted it should be a loan. As security the Professor reluctantly put up his most cherished possession—the collection of gems and minerals.

"Just a minute," said George Parkman, when his brother-in-law and partner Shaw casually mentioned this new loan in their office, "just a minute, there is an indecent repetition here! This security is no security; it is already mortgaged to me and others foolish enough to indulge that feckless man his vanities. Those things are not his to make over as he pleases again and again."

This affront to right dealing; this naïve fraud; this abuse of friendly generosity stirred inside George Parkman a monstrous outrage. When John Webster applied for the Harvard post, George Parkman had lent his good services to secure him the appointment. Through many years of slovenly and erratic conduct he and his family had, from their Christian fellow-feeling, sustained this ridiculous and unworthy man, if only for the sake of the College and his wife and children. Was this how such charity was repaid—the perpetration of a clumsy, underhand trick as though his friends and creditors were so many fools, to be carelessly palmed off with an airy wave of the hand? Well, he had forfeited the right to friendly consideration. If the man chose to behave like a common Irish rogue, he should be dealt with like one. In the alleys of the North End he had begun, and in the North End he should doubtless finish.

So George Parkman turned agency-man, pursuing his debtor wherever he could find him: at card-parties and concert suppers; at the Medical College annual inaugural address, directly in front of Webster's colleagues, Parkman's disconcertingly white false teeth barking reproaches in corners of the room. As Webster became evasive, so Parkman harried him wherever he could be found. During the first weeks of November he was bold enough to enter the lecture room (for, after all, he thought of it as Parkman property) and stand at the back, waiting for the class to end, with a silent expression of stony determination.

What was he to do? Only one way out of his predicament suggested itself. By the third week of the month he should have accumulated enough fees from lecture tickets to pay off the Doctor, though he had been depending on those sums to settle with the tradesmen who were descending on him with their bills and charges.

Then one afternoon Mr. Pettee, who collected the fees from the students and made them over to Webster's account, called on the Professor, looking sheepish and red in the face. After deducting a note due to Dr. Bigelow, there was $275 remaining from one book of tickets; near enough another two hundred from a further batch. But, well, Pettee stammered, Dr. Parkman had been to see him, asking, well demanding, the moneys be surrendered directly to him in settlement of the Professor's debt. Of course, rest assured, he had done no such thing and he had done his best to make the Doctor understand that he was certainly not authorised to pay the money to anyone but the instructor. And when he had told him he had already paid a sum over, Dr. Parkman had uttered something pretty hard such as "the Devil you have." It was too bad, Dr. Parkman added, that this had happened, for now he should be obliged to *distress* Dr. Webster and what was worse, his family. By this Seth Pettee imagined he meant some sort of legal proceedings, but he could not pass this on to the Professor, still less what Dr. Parkman had asked him to communicate; namely, that he thought Webster neither an upright nor an honourable man.

At the news of this latest indignity, a smarting

sense of impotence and humiliation rose inside John Webster. Was it not enough that poor Harriet should be forced to make sharp economies at home? She had even been obliged to go so far as to enter into secret commercial practice, buying brilliantly coloured and woven fabrics from the looms of St. Michael and Fayal and reselling them to dressmakers in Boston. If reports of her little business should ever become public, how would she bear the mortification? Though that would be nothing compared to any kind of ordeal in the courts.

A note bearing George Parkman's attacking hand arrived for the Professor at the College. It minced no words, threatening exposure and disgrace, the distraint of the law. A week later the Doctor arrived in person, walking directly into the Professor's back room while he was preparing a lecture as though he were some sort of tenant-at-will being threatened with eviction. Dr. Parkman did not even have the decency to wait until Littlefield was out of the way but proceeded directly to demand in a high, imperious tone that "something must be accomplished."

Very well, something would be accomplished. The visit had been on Monday the nineteenth. The following Friday the Professor called early in the morning at Dr. Parkman's house in Walnut Street to propose a meeting that afternoon. Some form of settlement was intimated. Later that same morning the anxious Mr. Pettee called again with a small but welcome check. "I shouldn't worry," said Webster to reassure his visitor, "Doctor Parkman is a peculiar sort of man; rather nervous, don't you know, subject to aberrations of mind. But you will have no further trouble with him now for I have settled with him." Mr. Pettee went away much relieved.

Could it be that the man had finally been chastened into meeting his obligations? Parkman wondered, as he set off for the College. He would not be surprised if he was to be palmed off yet again with some insipid and disingenuous pretext. But Webster's rather tense, solemn manner that morning suggested some change of demeanour. We shall see. First, to market to buy that lettuce for poor daughter Harriet, to quicken her appetite into life.

On that same Friday, late in the afternoon, while the last remains of autumn warmth hung in the air, Professor Webster walked away from the College and took himself to Brighams, where he ate a mutton chop for his supper. He next stopped in at Kidder's pharmacy to buy himself a bottle of cologne, after which (in the spirit of the new frugality) he took the omnibus back to Cambridge. That evening he and his wife walked the girls to a party at the Batchelders' and themselves went on to the Treadwells' for a lively game of whist with friends and neighbours. Nothing untoward punctuated the usual, scattered conversations, though there was too much dull technical talk of recent advances in mechanical ventilation for Harriet Webster's liking.

That night her husband confided in her. He had at last, he said, settled with Dr. Parkman, to the tune of $483 and some loose change, paid in person that very afternoon. The Doctor had taken it with his usual directness and without comment; had struck a line through the mortgage, promised to go to Cambridge to have it properly discharged and had peremptorily exited at speed. In the circumstances, and after all that had passed between them, Parkman implied, he was not inclined to delay for the sake of mere social formalities. And there was an end to it.

The following evening the Professor read aloud from Milton's *L'Allegro* and *Il Penseroso* to the family, together with the evening's guest, Miss Hodges, gathered in the parlour. The candlelight reflected off his spectacles as he drew himself up and began in his grandest declamatory style:

*Hence loathed Melancholy,*
  *Of Cerberus, and blackest midnight born,*
*In Stygian cave forlorn.*

## Debt: Skyrocket Jack

*'Mongst horrid shapes, and shrieks, and sights*
    *unholy,*
*Find out some uncouth cell . . .*

As the lines became more pastoral and travelled
through the realms of Mirth where "the milk-maid
singeth blithe, / And the mower whets his scythe,"
his voice became lower and the lyric cadences
seemed to the girls to resemble his flute, liquidly
legato. But *Il Penseroso* followed in antiphony:

*Hail divinest Melancholy,*
*Whose saintly visage is too bright*
*To hit the sense of human sight . . .*

And in keeping with the altered tone, the Professor's
voice turned diminuendo, oddly faltering at times,
Marianne thought. And when he read, near its close,

*And may at last my weary age*
*Find out the peaceful hermitage,*

she saw him in her mind's eye, truly grown ancient,
white-haired and infirm.

*The hairy gown and mossy cell,*
*Where I may sit and rightly spell*
*Of every star that Heaven doth show,*
*And every herb that sips the dew;*

*Till old experience do attain*
*To something like prophetic strain.*
*These pleasures melancholy give,*
*And I with thee will choose to live.*

A heavy silence followed before mirthful applause and Marianne's entering with the rainwater
Madeira.

Next morning, a Sunday, the weather had
turned sour and cool. Earlier rumours that Dr.
Parkman had disappeared were confirmed by
handbills liberally pasted about Cambridge. Surely, the Professor told his wife, as someone who had
seen the Doctor on the very day he had gone
missing, he should let the family know? Not this
morning, replied his wife, since his brother will be
at church.

After chapel, not in the North End but closer by
in Harvard Yard, the Professor took an early Sunday dinner and made his way in the cold rain to
Boston. Everywhere he went he announced what
had taken place the previous Friday: how Dr. Parkman had indeed come to see him; how he had been
paid what was due; how he had departed at speed
and that that was the last the Professor had seen of
him; how the Professor trusted, since Dr. Parkman
was such a man of his word, that he had indeed
cancelled the mortgage. He said this to Parkman's
nephew Mr. Blake at three; to Ephraim Littlefield
a few minutes later, rapping his cane on the ground

for emphasis; and he made the same announce-ment to the Reverend Francis Parkman at his house.

That family, increasingly desperate and anxious, was expecting something more than such a report delivered as it was, thought Francis, in so very business-like a manner. John Webster was a friend of so many years' standing. When his presence had been announced by the servant, their troubled gloom had momentarily lifted, for he had always been ready with words of kindness and sympathy. But his behaviour on this afternoon of all times was so peculiarly hasty that it verged on discourtesy.

The days petered out towards the holiday. The Professor was busy with his last classes at the College, but was at home at regular times for dinner and for tea. He played his flute; the girls sang; he tended to the garden where the grape-vines needed their autumn trimming. The whole College, on both sides of the Charles River, hummed with stories of the missing person. Yes, he had to tell colleagues and neighbours, he had seen him that Friday; yes, the police had of course searched the College but had found nothing that might help.

More handbills went up around town. The day before Thanksgiving the Professor was stopped with the girls at a toll-house on their way to a party at the Cunninghams' and observed a new notice. He read it aloud to them:

$1000 REWARD

Whereas no satisfactory information has been obtained respecting

DR. GEORGE PARKMAN

since the afternoon of Friday last and fears are entertained that he has been murdered, the above Reward will be paid for information which leads to the recovery of his body.

Robert G. Shaw

"Will it be found, Pa?" Catherine asked. "I'm sure I don't know, my dear," he replied, "everything is being done that may be." At the Cunninghams' some mischievous party asked, "Do you suppose, Dr. Webster, that as the last person to see Dr. Parkman you may yourself be under suspicion?" "Why," he retorted amiably enough, "do you imagine I *look* like a murderer?" Polite laughter rippled round the room.

Around eight o'clock in the evening of the day after Thanksgiving, Colonel Derastus Clapp, Officer Starkweather and Officer Spurr appeared at the garden gate of John Webster's house. He was seeing a guest out to the street with his usual cheery sounds of farewell.

"I'm sorry to be bothering you again, Doctor," said the detective, "but we need to go over the

College again and would deem it a great favour if you were present."

Clapp's courtesy was accompanied by enough firmness of manner to suggest that the Professor had no option, and he showed himself willing. Clapp pointed to the coach waiting a few yards down the street. The Professor went in the house, put on boots, coat and hat, and then got into the coach with the policeman.

They followed the Charles River east; the policemen and the Professor exchanged views on the controversial plan to bring the railroad to Cambridge, and then turned, inevitably, to all the tales flying about town of Dr. Parkman's whereabouts.

"There is a woman, a Mrs. Bent, who knows something about it, lives over there in Cambridge Port," said Webster. "Suppose we ride over there."

"Another time I'm sure we should," replied Clapp.

"Have I told you that I saw the Doctor, you know, that Friday?" And Clapp let him tell the story once again, adding that if the body and the cancelled mortgage were never found, he hoped the Professor would not be the loser.

At the Craigie Bridge the tide was down, revealing the greasy mud of the Charles, lit by the moon. It was there, the detective went on, that we looked for him, though a hat, you know, has been found in the Navy Yard where the tide might have carried it.

"This is surely not the way," interjected Webster

as the coach made a right turn on the Boston side of the bridge onto Brighton Street.

"The driver might be a bit green, I suppose, but he'll find his way."

A sudden silence descended on the inside of the coach. Officers Starkweather and Spurr, who had said little all the way, now said nothing and continued to look out the window unconcerned. Derastus Clapp looked steadily at Webster, who had lost colour and fallen uncharacteristically quiet.

The coach pulled up. It was Leverett Street jail. Mr. Clapp continued the courtesies.

"Gentlemen, I wish you would get out and come into the jail office a few moments."

Once inside, the policemen suddenly assumed a more formal manner—boots astride, hands behind their back. Webster turned to Clapp, who was standing behind him: "What does this mean?"

"Dr. Webster, you recollect that at the bridge I called your attention to soundings having been had above and below the bridge. We have been sounding elsewhere too, in and about the College, looking for the body of Dr. Parkman." He spoke now stenographically, in the manner of a policeman reporting to a magistrate. "We shall not look for his body any more; and you are in custody on a charge of the murder of Dr. Parkman."

"What, me?"

"Yes, you, sir."

At the words of the accusation, carrying with them a scriptural as well as a judicial force, John Webster lost his coherence, blurting out, half-sobbing, half-choking, "My family, my family, what will become of them?" And recovering himself for a moment, asked the detective to let them know where he was. Perhaps it would be kinder, the other replied, to spare them this night of sadness and trouble; allow them still to believe you are at the College helping with the search. It would not be wholly a deception because they must indeed go there shortly.

"And what of friends, may they not know of this?"

"They could not see you tonight in any event. I think we had better leave it until the morrow."

The Professor stood there, bewildered, wet-eyed, blinking behind the spectacles. A gold watch, a bunch of keys, two dollars and forty cents cash and an omnibus ticket were taken from him, dropped on a table, itemised, wrapped in a large handkerchief and locked away in the back office. With a hand about his shoulder, almost avuncular, but with a touch of constabular firmness at the knuckles, Starkweather led the prisoner in and sat him down.

After Derastus Clapp had gone to find the Marshal, the Professor asked for some water and when a jug was set beside him, rapidly emptied it. As if he hadn't heard the news the first time, or not believed what he had heard, he asked again, "Have they found the body of Dr. Parkman?"

Constable Starkweather gave the official reply: "I wish you would not ask me questions, Dr. Webster, for you know I cannot answer them."

He seemed not to hear, staring past the man: "But you might tell me *something*. Where did they find it? And did they find the whole body? How came they to suspect me?" And in a great rain of exclamations, the one dropping after the next: "Oh! My children, what will they do, what will they think of me? Where did they get the information?"

Starkweather attempted to stanch the flow with a question of his own. "Tell me, Doctor, did anyone but yourself have access to your private apartments?"

A sudden frown passed across his face, his brows knitted: "Nobody but the porter has such access."

He got up and walked up and down the small room, speeding up as he made the turns, wringing his hands; then suddenly stopping, he shouted, "That villain, I am a ruined man."

The Professor turned his body away from the policeman, and Starkweather thought he saw him reach inside his coat to the vest pocket and with a quick motion put his hand to his mouth. He sat down on the settee, his head on his hands, and very suddenly he threw his head back; his whole trunk began to tremble, the arms and legs twitching. Starkweather got up swiftly from his seat.

"Doctor, you haven't gone and taken anything, have you now?"

He shook his head, but his eyes were glassy and his body gripped by a red-faced convulsion, as though he were going into an epileptic fit. Starkweather lifted him off the couch and walked him over the floor. For some minutes the shuddering seemed to abate, but when Clapp returned and the Professor was told that he must now be committed, it began again with more violence. Holding on to Starkweather, he tried to lift himself off the chair but his legs gave and but for the policeman's grip on his arm he would have sprawled on the floor. Cummings, the turnkey, then put Webster's other arm about his shoulder and the two men dragged him, as gently as they could, down the stairs to the lock-up below. The space was lit with candles and a pair of oil lamps. An iron-barred gate swung open to admit the prisoner to a cell and swung back with an unlubricated squeal before shutting with a clang of finality.

About an hour later, the jail office filled up with grave-looking men. Jabez Pratt, the coroner, had been summoned, together with a number of medical gentlemen (some of them colleagues and ex-pupils of John Webster's), to examine the remains. But first they were to examine the prisoner. When he went below to the lock-up, Pratt was appalled.

Webster lay groaning face down on his bunk, mumbling unintelligibly. Two of the mutton-chop-whiskered men had to hold his plump body and roll it over. Dr. Gay spoke to him quietly, as if he were a child: "Now John, be calm, be calm, try and raise yourself, do."

"I cannot, I canner, I cannot," his whole face trembling with agitation and tears, the breaths coming short and unevenly.

"We shall help you, now let us try."

They took hold of him; a man at his legs, another two at his trunk, a fourth levering him up at his shoulders as if he were a boulder. Very suddenly and with unexpected force he sprang at one of them, his arm wrapping about the man's neck. It was not a gesture of violence but one of terror, accompanied by a pitiful wail. The arm went limp, was drawn away, and his body was heaved off the bunk to the floor and from the floor slipped upright, leaning against the iron door. Over and over sounded the lament: "What will become of my family?"

Paralysis resumed. The Professor slid to the floor and had to be dragged, as gently as was compatible with the urgency of the moment and the lateness of the hour, upstairs to the office and into a chair. In a still-muffled voice he asked for water but when it was brought, he was stricken again with what seemed to be a kind of hysterical palsy, something Dr. Gay had only seen before in

McLean Asylum. Webster reached for the glass, then struck it away, snatched at it once more and leaned his head forward slopping the water about his mouth and cheeks, swallowing nothing but blowing and biting at the glass so hard it had to be withdrawn in a sudden hurry lest he do himself some hurt.

"Come, this is all gammon," said Starkweather, losing his patience. Politer voices intervened, but there was a note of authority in their address.

"Pray calm yourself, do," said one of the be-whiskered men unknown to Webster, the county attorney, Samuel Parker, who was responsible for the committal. "We are not here to do you harm. But we have our duties to perform and amongst them is the investigation of what has been found at the College. Those remains, sir, demand an explanation, as you must appreciate, and we are sure you may help us find just such an explanation. Perhaps you might help us there even at this hour."

From somewhere came a small voice: "If I can, I will do so by all means."

"A coach stands at the door for us."

"But my friends, Mr. Dexter, Mr. Prescott."

"It is too late for friends tonight, Dr. Webster."

He buried his face in his hands once more. "My poor poor family."

For a moment Parker lost patience. "There is another family, you know, Dr. Webster, that has been in the greatest distress all of this week. We owe them some solicitude now and we owe duty to society as well as to ourselves. You know you will have ample opportunity to make any explanation you think fit and I hope to God, sir, you may explain the whole of this matter."

The turnkey and the jail-keeper each took one arm about his shoulders and pulled their prisoner into the coach. When it reached the Medical College, he was once more helped up the steps, his teeth chattering with the cold, but sweat pouring down his face. The little company waited at the door with a harsh east wind whipping about their heads, the policemen nervously glancing down the streets, expecting trouble at any time.

The Professor was taken to his own rooms, and there he seemed a little recovered. At least he could stand and speak, enough at any rate to warn the searchers in his private study to be careful with all the glassware and scientific valuables there. Drawers were pulled sharply out; those that stuck, smashed open with hatchets; papers and books scattered. "I don't know what they want there," he said amidst the splintering, "they will not find anything improper there."

From there the party went downstairs. The dark space was lit with flickering candles casting leaping shadows against the wall. Groups of men filled the room, murmuring to each other. The Professor was asked for his key to the privy and produced one that failed to fit. One of the men simply stood before him, arms folded across his chest in silent accusation. The trembling began again; Webster took off his spectacles, wiped them on a handkerchief, replaced them; then did the same thing all over. The furnace door was opened. Bones were pulled out from the ashes, some of them clinging to lumps of charred wood. "Put them back directly and leave things just as they are," shouted Coroner Pratt through the crowded gloom.

Out of the door and along the corridor to the trap-door the party went. Detective Clapp, Ephraim Littlefield and some others disappeared into the crawl space. After a few minutes a hand emerged holding something white and foul—a mess of viscera lying over a broad, flat bone. Webster wrenched his head from the sight; the rest of his body began again its terrible dance of shuddering and shaking. From his throat came noises of choking and gagging, pitiful cries for water, and when it was brought, the same violent shoving aside, then a leaning, snatching, snapping at the glass like something rabid and foaming.

There was nothing more to be said or done to him, not now. The turnkey, John Cummings, gently lifted him back into the coach and laid him on the back seat. On the ride back Webster spoke yet again of his family and huddled close to his jailor, soaking him with the bath of cold sweat that had seeped through his pants and coat. Carried back to his bunk in the cell that smelled of dust and despair, he lay with his head propped up on a bolster, and at one and then at two and then at two-thirty, the jailor looked in to see him immobile, spasms gone, body still, face turned up, eyes staring into the darkness. In the yellow glow of the jailor's candle he looked not so much dead as embalmed.

# 5
# Taking Stock:
# The Prisoner and the Public

It has never been easy to keep a secret in Boston, especially if that secret concerns mischief. Since the time of the Puritan Governors Bradford and Winthrop, a premium has been placed on publicity as a form of social cleansing. If a wrong has been done, it must have been done not just to individuals but to the community. So the whole congregation of the faithful has a right, a duty, to hear of the deed; to mark the wrongdoer; to accept his atonement; to pray for healing and the restoration of grace. Constantly aware that he was the inspector inspected, no one understood this better than Marshal Tukey. So he instituted the famous "shows" of pickpockets and other such riff-raff at his offices where good citizens could come and gawk and judge, or if the mood took them, upbraid and accuse. The essential thing was a vigorous humiliation, a modern pillory, something that would not be forgotten by the righteous and the unrighteous alike.

The Great Boston Murder, though, has generally been a different kind of show—more in the way of an interrupting ritual: something that pushes aside the quotidian; provokes a great many public utterances on the state of the times, demands sermons, editorials, predictions of doom, messages of redemption, Calvinist sound-bites. In all these commentaries the malefactor, especially the unlikely malefactor, is represented as the captive agent of the real criminal: Money. Professor William Douglas of Tufts University, who battered his greedy whore Robin Benedict to death in 1984, did so from desperation that he could no longer afford her. Charles Stuart, Newbury Street fursalesman, may have killed his pregnant wife in 1989 so that he might build his palace-in-the-air, an up-market restaurant, on the insurance proceeds. In 1850, God's appointed fulminators up and down the Commonwealth saw in the act of a Professor who would fecklessly destroy his honour, his reputation, his family, his life, all for a paltry few hundred dollars, the unmistakable warning of God to idolatrous Babylon.

On Saturday, December 1, 1849, a statue to the Antonine sophist Aristides was unveiled in Louisburg Square, at the topographical and moral center of Beacon Hill. His *Heroi Logi* is the peculiar autobiography of a man in whose daily life the spirit of Asclepius the healer constantly intervenes, saving the storm-tossed mortal from calamity. At the gracefully understated ceremony, a polite group of gentlemen in high hats and ladies in bonnets applauded (without removing their gloves) as a sheet dropped to reveal a peculiarly less-than-life-size sculpture of the spiritually directed diarist and orator.

On the same morning a crowd of men, many of them in mufflers and knitted caps, gathered about the front door of the Harvard Medical College. They were curious and noisy; some of them were angry. They had caught the trail of rumour as it had snaked its way about the city since the dawn hours, up from the river to the West End and down into Mayor Quincy's market, where the vendors of greenstuffs and pumpkins and the drovers of cattle met to exchange gossip over a mulled ale at the break of day. In no time at all the rumour had travelled on past the market down into the Irish North End where the memory of Dr. Parkman was suddenly transformed from that of an exacting landlord into a sainted benefactor. Folk remembered acts of kindness: a bottle of crimson linctus brought for a small child with a ragged cough; the surprising appearance of men sent to repair a leaking roof and who, when finished, left no bill.

If the Doctor now seemed transfigured as the Healer, the Medical College where, it was said, pieces of him had been found, was plainly a place of cold death and hot damnation. Everyone knew that bodies had been pried from fresh graves—yes, and the bodies of the poor, even children, from Copp's Hill and the Neck—to supply the anato-mists' tables. Now there were not enough even of the dead (at any rate those clean of the Asiatic cholera), so the dark doctors had turned to the living for their inventory. A place for the Devil's work! Down with it; sack it; tear it asunder; let fire consume its poisons!

At eight o'clock in the morning, when Marshal Tukey and his officers had to use their sticks to enter the building, there were already fifty irate people, as yet content to jostle and shove. By mid-day there were five hundred, and the noise was more ominous; by the late afternoon a huge crowd of two thousand jammed outside the gates and down North Grove Street all the way to Cambridge Street. Sticks and fists were being waved about. It was too ugly for the Marshal's fifty policemen to contain even if every last one of them was taken off his beat, delivering the rest of the city to villains. So the Marshal went to see Mayor Quincy and Gover-nor Briggs and had their assent to mobilise the militia at Roxbury that night. As darkness fell, he periodically lifted his face and sniffed the night air, like a big animal, alert for a whiff of woodsmoke.

He knew, after all, what the public did not yet know, though it could not long remain hidden. He had seen what they had not seen. He supposed himself a hard enough man, the Marshal did, and in his time he had looked at things that would make other men swoon away. He had lived too long in the company of vice and cruelty, and knew pretty much what devilry they could do. But when he thought of the grisly slop he had seen yesterday night and again today his gorge rose. As he understood the meaning of the word "sensation," it was something a man felt, not reflected on; something that crawled on his neck or swam in the tank of his belly. Well, this was a sensation alright, something he could apprehend but not comprehend.

Thank God for Coroner Pratt; he was not a man to fool around with niceties, but a true professional man after his fashion. His own men, he thought, liked it better upstairs, emptying desks, listening to Littlefield collect clues for them: the spots on the stairwell, rags and cloths and the like. But it was downstairs, in that dark, oppressive place, that the real business had got done. Once some lamps were lit, Mr. Pratt had just reached his arm into the furnace slag and pulled out pieces of bone: a piece of jawbone, with mineral teeth all fused together by the fire and sticking to a blackened lump of wood; a long grey bone he thought a tibia; a finger; a toe; odd teeth. He would bend and rise, bend and rise, his whole arm inside the dead oven as bits of the man were extracted.

Mr. Eaton had run off to puke but all of this was nothing to what followed. It was Fuller who found it, the tea-chest. It had been sitting there all week, hadn't it, delivered by the expressman Sawin, full of minerals and a couple of bags of tan that the Professor said he was using for an experiment with leather. Fuller had smelled something bad, something deeper and sweeter and fouler than any minerals, and had reached down and when his fingers had grasped something cold and repellent had yelled for his boss like a child in pain. When the box was emptied they were staring at a headless trunk. For a fleeting second the Marshal thought of prints he had seen of Antique torsos, their necks and rumps taken off by the casual accidents of time. What a piece of work is man! But this was hackabout trash, a sallow length of flesh and bone with a great mat of hair clinging to the back, an inch thick, gray and curling. Inside the body cavity were a lung, a kidney, the spleen—offal—and shoved into its cage was a whole thigh, held hanging by a cord.

After that it was difficult to pay attention to the details: the bowie knife in the chest with the tan and potash; a second knife found upstairs, this one exotic-looking, with a curved blade and a silver hasp; the saw, suspiciously free of stain or spot, that Starkweather brought down from the upstairs laboratory; the stained pieces of towel brought in by the relentless Littlefield.

The Marshal thought again of the weeping piece of misery he had seen in the jail last night. Was such as he capable of *this*? Would anyone believe it?

## Taking Stock: The Prisoner and the Public

The Coroner's jury certainly believed it. That afternoon and the following morning they were brought to the College to look at the remains; all of them, Brewster the printer, Restleray the chemist and the rest, evidently men of strong stomachs. A medical committee, some of them like Winslow Lewis close acquaintances and ex-students of John Webster. The pathologists, anatomists, chemists and dentists studied what there was to study: bones, teeth, organs, hair; also stains, blotches, chemicals. They separated them, classified them, labelled them, reported on them. The jury listened to their presentation in private but not quite as privately as they imagined: a resourceful team of penny-press reporters had bribed their way into the cellar beneath the ward room and were listening attentively at an air vent when they were caught; one sleuth sped away, the other was dragged before Coroner Pratt, who gave him a severe dressing-down.

For better security the Coroner's hearing was removed to the Court-house, where on December 14, two weeks following the discovery of the remains, they were declared to be those of Dr. George Parkman. A further declaration was made, stating that the deceased had met his end "by blow or blows, wound or wounds . . . inflicted upon him by the hands of said Doctor John Webster, by whom he was killed."

·    ·    ·

And what, in the meantime, had happened to the two doctors?

The mortal remains of Dr. George Parkman had been given the funeral rites on December 6. A long train of carriages had followed the hearse on which lay a coffin, lead-lined within, silver-plated without. Reporters had scrambled along the procession not scrupling as to whom they asked, or for that matter who answered, their questions. Many were shut out from Trinity Church on Summer Street, its rusticated masonry and crenellated tower protecting the coffin from vulgar intruders, and then its crypt offering the coffin a resting place.

The mortal part of Dr. John Webster had rallied from the prostration of arrest, accusation and detention. Turnkey Cummings and Jailor Leighton were quite surprised, given their fresh memory of the choking sobs of the night of November 30, that nothing much other than an occasional buzz-like snore came from their most distinguished prisoner's cell. Though he had to withstand the inevitable chaffing from the many rogues who were in the Leverett Street lock-up pending trial, he often seemed in better spirits than they.

By the Monday following his ordeal, the Professor was already making arrangements for his own housekeeping and for sustaining his role as a

Boston benefactor by nourishing his fellow inmates (however disrespectful) with his unwanted victuals.

In the evening he wrote to his daughter:

My Dearest Marianne,

I wrote mamma yesterday and Mr. C[unningham] who was here this morning told me he had sent it out. I had a good sleep last night and dreamt of you all. I got my clothes off for the first time and awoke in the morning quite hungry. It was a long time before my breakfast from Parkers came; and it relished I can assure you. At one o'clock I was notified I must appear at the Court Room. All was arranged with great regard to my comfort and avoidance of publicity and this first ceremony went off better than I had anticipated. On my return I had a bit of turkey and rice from Parkers. They send much more than I can eat and I have directed the steward to distribute the surplus to any poor ones here.

If you will send me a small cannister of tea, I can make my own. A little pepper, I may want some day; you can put it up with some bundle. I would send the dirty clothes but they were taken to dry and have not been returned. Half a dozen Rochford powders I should like. Tell mamma *not to open* the little bundle I gave her the other day but to keep it just as she received it. Hope you will soon be cheered by receipt of letters from Fayal. With many kisses to you all.

Good night from
Your afft. father

P.S. My tongue troubles me yet, very much, and I must have bitten it in my distress, the other night; it is painful and swollen, affecting my speech somewhat.

Perhaps his swollen tongue and thickened speech were the reason why he had had so little to tell Franklin Dexter, his kinsman and attorney, when the first visits had been allowed on Saturday. The signs of trauma—disarrayed clothes, a bad odour of fear and cold sweat—were still written on John Webster, but given the ordeal to which he had been subjected, the lawyer thought, any man, including himself, would have looked as bad. Besides, what was alleged was absolutely inconceivable; a monstrous and abominable tissue of circumstantial evidence, of unsupported innuendos and defamatory incriminations. Let him recover himself a little, receive some nourishment and the succour and loyalty of friends and family, and all would surely be explained. "Those bones are no more Doctor Parkman's than they are my own," Webster had told Dexter, and it could hardly be astonishing to discover dismembered cadavers in a medical college.

The family arrived, wife and elder daughters managing to contain their misery and horror for the sake of Papa—who remained, as they insisted to anyone they thought doubted it, an *angel*—the youngest, Catherine, quavering on the edge of tears. They brought him comforts and dainties;

dried flowers and a little fruit cake, dark with spiced rind and molasses. As days passed he seemed altogether changed again into something resembling their pudgily amiable sentimental father. He asked them about the neighbours, the garden, Harvard gossip, as if he were confined to an infirmary bed and expecting an early recovery and discharge.

Nor had Harvard yet disowned him. A procession of his learned colleagues made its way to the Leverett Street jail: not least President Sparks, Henry Wadsworth Longfellow, and Edward Everett, who wrote to his friend Sidney Brooks:

It is beyond all comparison the most painful event in our domestic history. Dr. Webster was my classmate, my playmate from a period still earlier. I have known him from our earliest boyhood. His family, a wife and three daughters are most amicable and accomplished persons: universal favorites.

And in the weeks to Christmas, when the Boston newspapers (all fifteen of them) were busy speculating merely on the degree of the prisoner's guilt, John Sibley, the College librarian, reported that "the professors pooh at the mere supposition that he is guilty." They knew him too well, his "artlessness and unfamiliarity with crime of any kind." More important, "his uniform tenor of conduct since the disappearance of Doctor Parkman has been such that the excitement, the melancholy, the aghastness of everybody are incredible." Yet he added, dolefully, "The vicinity of the Medical College, State Street, the newspaper offices are crowded and thronged. People cannot eat; they feel sick."

Though not yet delivered to the sack, the College was definitely in a state of siege. Life had become intolerable, the faculty having to run a gauntlet of jeers and curses to get in at the front door; snouty faces pressed against the windows; the occasional projectile flung hard at the window panes. Meeting at Dr. Jacob Bigelow's house, the beleaguered professors decided to call a recess of three days to allow the inflamed situation to cool. They would mourn the loss of their benefactor and at the same time recover their own composure. What were they to do? What were they to believe? As colleagues and friends who had known John Webster for more than twenty years, had tolerated his petulant eccentricities, had warmed to his boyish enthusiasms for fossils and ancient skeletons, they could not imagine him to have done such a thing. To suppose that he had would mean setting their human understanding at naught; recognising that they too (for how different were they?) might be capable of such a deed, or searching through George Parkman's publications on mental disorders for signs of the double-personality that could present a meek and cordial face to the world and,

on occasion, assume another countenance of unspeakable ugliness and rage.

And yet, they were men of science. Certain
evidence had been presented; they could not deny
it. Men of serious repute and professional distinction had given their opinion against the Professor.
(Though they mistrusted Charles Jackson for trying to rob Dr. Morton of the credit for inventing
anaesthetic ether). At any rate, it was their judgement that had become the verdict of the Coroner's
Court. The thing to do, Dean Holmes thought,
would be to appoint Dr. Horsford as a substitute
lecturer, so that the students would not suffer,
without in any way compromising their colleague's
presumption of innocence. If they could not stand
against the newspapers' rush to judgement, who
then could be relied on to defend the unim-
peached integrity of the accused? "What is a character worth?" wrote Nahum Capen to Horace
Mann just before Christmas,

if by the breath of slander or by the floating uncertainty
of suspicion it may instantly be changed from integrity
to perfidy, from purity to corruption, from refinement
to barbarity and from the highest sentiments of honor
and religion to the lowest capacity of the wolf and the
bloodhound! What is character—if people are ready
without fears and doubts to translate the faithful teacher
to the felon's cell; the good citizen to the lowest depths
of shameless crime; the friend to the place of the demon
and to transform the man to the monster?

In Cambridge drawing-rooms it was keenly felt that much of this guilt by implication, by untested association, was Boston's doing. Never had the two banks of the Charles seemed more widely separated. On the north side, humanity, learning, generosity, prudence, an aristocracy of honour and morality; on the south side, a shrinking ground of decency assailed on all sides by creatures from the gutter—the reptiles of the penny-press, the hucksters of rumour and innuendo, the noisy, gaudy habitués of the Melodeon, the enthusiasts of the gallows, the scoundrels and fast-driving enforcers of Marshal Tukey's world.

On both sides of the river, though, the deed stained the snows of the holiday season. Last year had been especially festive, with sleighing at the Neck and the ice so solid that revellers could skate all the way from Long Wharf to Spectacle Island. Count Papanti's All-Age Balls, featuring the cotillion, the polka and the waltz, had been especially brilliant. This year, alas, "Caper City" had lost its taste for merriment, at least in polite society. Mrs. Harrison Gray Otis's Dancing Academy in Tremont Street went into recess. Private parties were put off, musical gaiety silenced; people withdrew into their own parlours, where they took extraordinary care not to mention the names of Parkman and Webster. There was, as one commentator put it, "a general check on hilarity."

## Taking Stock: The Prisoner and the Public

In the family circle of the Prescotts, the mood was particularly gloomy because Mrs. Prescott and Mrs. Webster were half-sisters. Father and son Prescott went regularly to see the prisoner and to Cambridge to offer what comfort they could to the Webster women who, among other sorrows, were now seriously distressed for their living and were taking in sewing to make ends meet. Young William the historian was asked by his brother for his understanding if the entertainment planned to greet his return from Europe was of a modest and intimate kind, given the sadness and anxiety of the time.

For John Webster's extended family nothing was more urgent than attending to his defence and procuring him the best possible counsel. There was no shilly-shallying on this account. The greatest attorneys of the Commonwealth, indeed the greatest *men* of the Commonwealth, were directly addressed by Franklin Dexter, to whom all doors on Beacon Hill were habitually open.

When it was learned that such as Daniel Webster the Orator and Rufus Choate had been approached, two kinds of conclusions were drawn by two kinds of commentators. One group admired the boldness of the action, taking it as a sign of a sturdy belief in the Professor's innocence. The other party, growing more numerous with the weeks that intervened between the Grand Jury indictment and the trial, took a less generous view, assuming the cause was so desperate and the evidence so damning that nothing short of high legal wizardry (for which the likes of Choate were famous) could possibly rescue the Professor from the rope.

Both gentlemen declined the honour. Daniel Webster, whose black eyes set beneath "precipice brows" Carlyle had compared to "anthracite furnaces needing only to be *blown,*" seemed to be dwelling in a cloud of melancholy. The year before he had lost two children, a girl to tuberculosis, a son to the Mexican War. Now he felt (correctly) that he was about to lose his standing with the citizens of the Commonwealth. Years of exposure to the complicated and laborious procedures of state in Washington had stripped him of many of the high certainties esteemed by the Massachusetts voters. To the dismay and wrath of Free-Soilers, Abolitionists and Transcendentalists, he was about to make his peace with Henry Clay's compromise to support a Fugitive Law that would uphold the right of arrest of runaway slaves in free states. The preservation of the Union (not to mention the sanctity of property) he now set above the execution of virtue. A long speech was being written. He knew what was in store for him; how Garrison and Phillips would flay him in the columns of the *Liberator.* He felt old and tired and needed to store his winter energy.

Rufus Choate seemed more promising. His histrionic gifts (in a city where that quality was much admired on stage, in pulpit and in print) were unsurpassed. His whole person was a carefully organised dramatic spectacle: the five overcoats that he removed one by one in court; the unattended black hair that fell over the dazzlingly ugly face; the astonishing knee jerks and muscular exertions that bewitched the jury; the melodies of the voice and the lethal sharpness that punctuated his cross-examinations. The great Choate could do anything. He had, after all, persuaded a jury that a man accused of murdering his wife had done it in his sleep and that a somnambulist could not, by definition, be guilty of malice aforethought.

But the mighty Choate (who respected Franklin Dexter as a court-room adversary to whom, on occasion, he had even lost the odd case) had his doubts. Anticipating Dexter's offer, he had himself spoken to Littlefield, considered the evidence and the Professor's claims and decided that he must concede that Dr. Parkman had indeed met his death in the Professor's laboratory. Just how that came about was then for the prosecution to show, and it would, he thought, be no simple matter. Indeed, to show beyond any reasonable doubt that the death had been a premeditated act of cold-blooded murder would, he reckoned, be hard, if not impossible. He would ensure that it would be so. But they had to get the matter of the body behind them; for how (he later told Sumner), other than supposing Parkman had gone into Webster's private room, shaken himself into several pieces and then distributed them about the building, could one conceivably imagine they got to such places as tea-chests and furnaces and privy vaults?

Dexter was despondent. Such an admission, he knew, would never be given nor indeed should be sought. John Webster was less subtle than Choate. He had never swerved from his adamant insistence that the last he had seen of Parkman was his rushed exit from the laboratory holding the money he had been paid; that he had no idea whatever how the remains, if they were indeed Parkman's, came to be on the premises. Even now he was beginning to prepare notes explaining everything the Coroner's jury had found so compromising. So much of his defence had to rest on the absolute discrepancy between the vileness of the crime and the normality of his conduct in the week following the disappearance. How could that now be set at naught by such a retraction? No, it was unthinkable, even at the cost of doing without Choate.

No recourse was left but to have counsel appointed by the court. Not that this put John Webster in the hands of unknown or untested persons. Shown a list of attorneys, he selected two of the best known and respected: Judge Pliny Merrick (Harvard Class of 1814), a long-faced, elegant, sober fellow who had left the Court of Common Pleas to become President of the Nashua and Wor-

cester Rail Road and had just now returned to the
bar; and as his second counsel, Edward Sohier,
called Ned by everyone in Boston, who followed
Choate in the school of carefully disarrayed dress
and slouching manners, the better to spring on the
unprepared witness.

When they came to see him twice or more a
week, the Professor seemed still to have great difficulty in adding much, indeed anything, to the
simple, unequivocal outline of his recollection. But
on paper his recall was more elaborate, his speculations bolder. Before the trial in March he would
give to his attorneys nearly two hundred pages of
such details outlining an entire strategy for the
defence.

He sat in his cell nibbling on cheese, sipping the
Madeira brought him by the Longfellows, scribbling this and that as things occurred to him. The
real Webster was protected from the public view
by the walls and bars of the Leverett Street jail;
some sort of Webster-figure had already been
tried, exposed, pelted with excoriation in the
press. The author of *The Boston Tragedy* had already decided that "a black and appalling case of
premeditated murder" had been done; that Governor Briggs already knew it to be so and had said as
much; that there was the clearest and most instruc-
tive contrast between the victim, famously frugal
and punctilious, and his killer, a man of extravagance, negligence "and total want of economy,"

whose pitiful inadequacies to his responsibilities had made him a lunatic and a murderer.

The bill of indictment, handed to the accused (who had not been allowed to appear on his own behalf) put it differently; namely that

John White Webster with a certain knife which he then and there in his right hand had held, the said George Parkman then and there feloniously willfully and of his malice aforethought did strike, beat and kick upon the head, breast, back and belly, sides and other parts of him, the said George Parkman and then and there feloniously willfully and with malice aforethought did cast and throw the said George Parkman down unto and upon the floor with great force and violence there giving unto the said George Parkman then and there as well as by the beating, stabbing, striking and kicking of him several mortal wounds and bruises in and upon the head, breast, belly and other sides of the body . . . of which said mortal strokes, wounds and bruises he the said George Parkman then and there instantly died.

# 6

# Accounts Rendered: Lawyers, Doctors and Other Solid Citizens

George Bemis, attorney-at-law, bachelor, who lived comfortably with his sickly father, and was bothered from time to time by a tearing, bloody cough, wondered: Ought he to take the case? It was, he supposed, a grand opportunity to make a mark. The Reverend Francis Parkman had, after all, sought him out personally, flattered him as "the pre-eminent among our criminal lawyers." Now why had he done that when the case went directly to the Attorney General unless he had some misgivings about friend John Clifford's capacities that way? He could understand that; there was something too easy about the man's manner, indeed about his whole career. If he had made the awful mistake of graduating from Brown, rather than Harvard, Clifford had made up for it by being close to the ubiquitous, the personable, Edward Everett: in Boston Governor Everett, in Cambridge

President Everett. And in case he should need a leg up on pedigree he had taken care to marry a descendant of Myles Standish the Pilgrim. Little wonder he had done so well, advancing relentlessly from his New Bedford law practice to district attorney of southern Massachusetts. The defunct office of Attorney General of the Commonwealth had been revived expressly for him. So why should he do this paragon's business for him when he would supply the toil and Clifford would doubtless reap the reward?

Then again could he afford not to take it? For he needed his independence, and only a modicum of money and respect could assure him of it. A thousand dollars was not a mean sum. And if not he, then who else? *Someone,* perhaps an inferior, unworthy fellow eager enough to please Attorney General Clifford and ingratiate himself with the Chief Justice (who *loved* prosecuting counsels). Hang it, it was the old story: his suspicions of himself as a nullity, as a walking professional convenience, as one dependent on the whims and leavings of this and that person.

Bemis's favourite cross-examinee was himself, and often enough a casuistical, slippery witness he proved to be. Last birthday, aged thirty-three and feeling already jaded over breakfast, he offered to his diary an unconvincing explanation for noticing the event at all.

I have a right or rather an obligation to notice it—to enquire wherefore I came into the world and whether I have lived accordingly. And in this morning dull meditations before rising (dull perhaps because of the heaviness and sleeplessness of the flesh)—I could hardly get any light or a clear view of the subject. I hoped for better things and prayed for them but with a dull desire and a somnolent hope. Heaven help me to better aspirations! Let me not live to take care of the body and obey any mechanical task that accident and professional routine impose upon me! Let me not live to forfeit free wishing and a constantly progressive course. As if the accumulation of money or the achievements of professional reputation were the terminus of my aims! Better to throw all accumulations and expectancies into the sea and live dependent upon manual toil so that I could keep myself alive and spiritually growing! Better be neglected and dishonored of all the forensic gladiators and the judicial theater than share with them all an enslaving and debasing craft!

Well, then, why should he jump when Mr. Clifford blew his whistle? Did he not value more his family hearth of brothers and sisters, all so amiable—"the pleasures of listening to music and enjoying sociability." Yes, he understood well enough Thoreau's praise of the blessings of simplicity; even the ecstatics at Brook Farm were, after all, embarked on an honourable enterprise:

the quest for harmony free from the selfishness of property. When did he feel more peaceful and blessed himself than sitting in Mrs. Whipple's salon with Sumner, Emerson and Garrison, surrounded by men of courage and integrity who cared not a fig for the niceties of society, for such things as diplomacy and manoeuvre, who walked the straight road and spoke their minds?

Ah, if only he could see his way clear to follow them. But it was, when he reflected a bit, not that simple. This Webster case: "Prudence bids me throw it off; ambition and professional interest resist." And after all, "pecuniary independence absolves me from the necessity of calling upon my father in his declining years or narrowing my brothers' and sisters' hope of competency." So perhaps, then, the unselfish thing, however distasteful, would be to step in when bidden.

January 27, 1850: "Ought I not to lend my talents to aid the State in a trial most searchingly affecting its criminal judicature? That I should be vain of proving a man guilty of murder, Heaven forbid! Or can I be willing to triumph professionally when the stake is life to the criminal and separation and perpetual peace to his family. Only if I may represent impartial justice in the person of the State, Christianity."

February 19, 1850: "I begin to see my name paraded in the newspapers as associate counsel in the Webster case. Yet my hearty blood runs cold.

How can I quicken it into activity? How make myself spontaneous and free and hopeful of enjoyment as when a boy? Will company do it? I make some considerable sacrifice, say half my evenings, in that view. Will change of habit and life? I dread that—travelling, for example—how uncomfortable to leave all those nooks and corners in which I am accustomed to nestle now. My care for nothing; my hotel, my solitary (femaleless) promenades, my free and easy office with its after-dinner and evening rocking chair—my Saturday and Sunday routine. Yet the prospect looks unpromising. How few friends? How little love to depend on?"

There was nothing for it. They all meant him to do it. Every time he set foot on the Long Path on the Common they all congratulated him on it. Even that great creature Chief Justice Shaw had turned his ghastly aspect on him and appeared to smile or at least not to scowl. He had better get to his books. Only three weeks to the trial. Damn that wretched cough!

Boston Doric, the usual thing: a pompous colonnade, a lofty pediment, a daunting flight of steps; not a temple but a Court-house. Before it, an uncountable number of bodies and faces, hats and bonnets, noses red and cheeks raw in the biting March wind, jammed closer together than propriety or custom sanctioned, bound by a single

determination: to get in. Holding a shifting, sway-
ing, bulging boundary is a small number of men in
uniform—a few of them on horseback, some of
them with their revolvers visible. The Marshal is
not among them, for he is to be a witness and has to
attend to the impression he must make; Colonel
Clapp, Officer Starkweather and others likewise
rehearse the manner of candid virtue their chief
has required of all his men for their day in court.

Sixty thousand would see the trial of John White
Webster; statistically nearly half the population of
Boston, but in reality a mass of the curious and
excited drawn from all over the state, all over the
country and even farther than that. Reporters had
been assigned from Berlin, Prussia, and Berlin,
New Hampshire; from York and New York. It was
the age, after all, of the temerity of professionals;
when science and *Bildung* were claiming to re-
fashion the nature of modernity. How then could
the public miss an occasion to see those claims so
outrageously abused; to see the Professor-killer
with the added dramatic possibility of his own
impending punishment?

The Boston police and the magistracy were becoming accustomed to the management of crowds
and thought they recognised the delicate boundary
that separated a crowd from a mob. What all these
people craved, they reasoned, was a taste of nov-
elty and spectacle. The same enthusiasts had
trooped to the Melodeon to see Mr. John Whipple

present his Grand Exhibition of the Wonders of Optical Science including Burr's Seven Mile Mirror. Nothing too prolonged or too profound was wanted; just a glimpse of Fanny Kemble, a song from Jenny Lind would do for bragging rights in the tavern or over morning muffins. In this spirit of turnstile democracy, the police were instructed to ensure a good even flow in the public galleries. Every ten minutes one ticketed crowd would rise amidst shuffling of benches and tramping of boots, to be replaced by another as the proceedings continued below uninterrupted if not undisturbed. After a day of this traffic even counsels and witnesses became accustomed to this mobile human scenery, standing and sitting, exiting and entering, murmuring and shushing.

Everyone in the court-room was acutely conscious of being on public view. When John Webster was brought in, he managed gracious smiles and even occasional handshakes for recognised friends, colleagues, kin, all those who had sustained him in his ordeal and who would now, God willing, see their faith vindicated. To some he seemed offensively jaunty. His gait as he walked to the dock, the reporter from the *New York Daily Globe* noted, "was light and elastic," suggesting good form in body and spirits. (Though the same writer added, for good measure, that "the physiognomist would note a countenance suggesting strong animal passions: high cheek-bones, a mouth with compressed lips, the forehead angular, rather low and partially retreating.")

Their Honours, the Chief Justices of the Supreme Court of the Commonwealth, were no more immune from the sense of public spectacle; indeed, they consciously reinforced it. Associate Justices Wilde, Dewey and Metcalf—the first, octogenarian, sombre and courtly; the second, squat, pugnacious and economically packed into his robes; the third, a threateningly attentive figure, a listener rather than a talker, as befitted someone whose career had been built as official reporter for the bench—were all supporters to their Chief; all sticks to lean against the great stone weight of his alarming, mountainous presence. It was not so much that Lemuel Shaw was physically imposing; it was just that his implacable manner made him seem so. Reminiscent of the omnipotent hanging judges of Hanoverian England, he needed no powdered, curled, falling white wig to assert his authority. A thatch of coarse hair, a startlingly ill-favoured countenance, a staring, forward way, an unbreachable sense of self-righteousness were quite enough to silence presumptuous counsels (especially presumptuous defending counsels) and strike terror into the heart of the accused. He sat like a great warty toad at the centre of the bench—immovable, unblinking, broad nostrils occasionally flaring at the suggestion of some impropriety, embodying in his bulk the very weight of justice.

At a time when both the deterrent efficacy and the moral legitimacy of capital punishment had been called into question, Chief Justice Shaw had no doubts about the matter. Indeed, he was prepared to thrust his certainty on juries, even on prosecuting attorneys, who showed themselves hesitant in the discharge of their duty. When the poor imbecile Pierson had been convicted of murdering his wife and two children in Wilmington the previous year, the jury had expressly and unanimously recommended clemency, yet Lemuel Shaw had no hesitation in overruling their squeamishness and sending the murderer to the noose. He had always lived his life in rectitude (even stories that he had been punished at Harvard for throwing snowballs turned out to be groundless), and he saw no reason why those who had violated the law ought not to reap the consequences.

So the Honourable Mr. Pliny Merrick (whose physiognomy, as much as his name, suggested some benign Roman consul), long-faced and elaborately courteous, and Mr. Edward Sohier (in superbly eccentric mustard vest), both knew they had their work cut out in defence. On March 18, a day before the trial, they had gone to the jail a last time to ask Dr. Webster (no longer Professor since he had resigned his chair following the indictment), if there was, perhaps, something he had omitted to tell them; something that had either weighed on, or indeed just slipped, his mind, as these things might. Something, anything of conceivable significance to the case?

"No, no," returned John Webster, "it is all there in the papers you have from me, enough I should think for you gentlemen?"

The gentlemen looked briefly at one another. Not enough, their exchange of glances said; too much yet, two hundred pages and more of Dr. Webster's instructions on how to construct the defence, and yet, they could not help feel, not enough.

It was an extraordinary document, really, they readily admitted. They could not recall any client in a similar position having so much to say on his account, so many minute details to correct, so many plausible explanations to dismiss what the prosecution was likely to suggest might be incriminating. The locking and bolting of his doors during the days after Dr. Parkman's disappearance, for example? Well, many of his colleagues knew that he habitually did so when he had to prepare a lecture or a demonstration. Dr. Warren always did likewise in his time. John Blake, student, 66 State Street, Boston, could affirm this. The spots on the floor and stairwell? Nitric acid used in his experiments, nothing more sinister. The business with the big wooden box found on the Saturday? Well, the fact that it had lain outside the lower laboratory all that week quite unconcealed was surely evidence that until *something foreign* had been introduced it was quite innocuous. After all, what had it held other than his chemical vessels he used at home in Cambridge, packed up for him and sent into Boston. The bags of tan? They had been sent expressly by a Mr. Southwick of Sutton Place so that he could follow, experimentally, a new process of treating leather. One of the skins would in all probability still be found in the woodhouse at home. The Turkish yataghan knife? An item he had brought from home that he commonly used to cut new corks for bottles and models of crystals and the like to display their mineralogical and chemical structure. The potash? Littlefield had procured it, not on his account either.

Yes, with his help, his counsel could cast doubt on the alleged motive, raise further doubts on Dr. Parkman's settled state of mind. Hadn't someone at Appleton's, the organ builders, mentioned how odd the Doctor had looked when he came to see the work being done for the lunatic asylum chapel? And if he certainly had taken to dunning Webster for the return of the loan, he had actually consented to his reselling or re-pledging the mineral collection. As for the money used to pay off the debt that Friday, he had saved it little by little at home expressly for that purpose.

To be sure, he could not explain how those body parts ended up on his premises. But was he required to do so? Given the presumption of innocence was it rather not incumbent on the Government to prove that they had come to be there by his particular agency?

Not that he was imputing *anything* you understand, but there was surely another set of connecting circumstances that could be presented with as much credibility as those weighing against him? Who, other than himself, had access through keys to all the chambers leading from his lecture room and down to the lower laboratory? Why the janitor of course. The Coroner's Court and the Grand Jury had been impressed with the fact that whoever had dismembered the body showed definite expertise in dissection. Well, he had not opened a body in twenty years. Littlefield, on the other hand, "had seen hundreds of bodies cut up, and attended post mortem examinations for years; indeed might be called an *expert*. He knew the ways and difficulties of separating joints, the sternum and so forth, knew how to prevent blood flowing and could no doubt cut up a body more *scientifically* than I."

The ways in which simple acts of generosity could be turned against him! That turkey for example, Sawin could testify how Webster was in the habit of giving birds at the holiday time. And though the janitor denies it, he had given him something each year, last year a dressing gown used in lectures. Could he be relied on? Judge Merrick ought to whittle away at the man's character; bring out his many acts of negligence; the arguments on that account they had had; his intemperance, not to mention his wife's!

He didn't say that Littlefield had done the deed himself. The key to it all was his long career as a resurrectionist; his notorious recklessness about getting subjects. There was that body of a young girl brought from New Hampshire that suddenly appeared in the College last year. Resurrectionists, after all, would do anything in these hard times to procure their income. Many cut off heads and sold those separately to specialists in optics or other superior organs. He would do things that no one else would touch, would Littlefield. Why, for two hundred dollars he had cleared out all the bodies that had accumulated in the vaults of the old College before it had moved to the new site; something no ordinary sensibility could stomach.

So in all likelihood Littlefield had brought the body to the College as a specimen to sell to the students, discovered whom he had acquired and in a funk had cut him apart and tried to burn the remnants. When he discovered that would take too long, he needed some other place to discard the cadaver. The dissecting-room vault was too obvious, but since he knew where the key to the privy was kept he would have no difficulty in using that instead. Indeed, now he came to think of it, there were many times that the janitor must have used the privy because Dr. Webster so often found the door unlocked when he distinctly remembered locking it.

Was this account, after all, any less probable than Webster's doing the deed by daylight in a room where he might have been interrupted by students, or attempting to burn the body when the smell would have advertised the deed throughout the building? Surely Judge Merrick could make much of a contrast in character, especially since there had been such an effort to blacken Webster's in the press and since he had had no opportunity to defend himself? Mr. Clifford, so well known to the family, surely would not stoop to such defamation in an attempt to create a portrait of a murderer? But perhaps counsel could, for the jury, paint a different portrait: the true likeness? "It can be fully proved," he wrote, "that I have been a devoted and affectionate father and that my happiness was centered in my home—my habits of instruction, reading with my family are known to many. Witnesses to this I can give a long list of. I am more anxious to save the feelings of my family and friends than for almost anything else."

No wonder Dr. Webster had an air of impending exoneration about him as he waited for the proceedings to begin. He had set it out, all the points of incrimination explained and refuted one by one and if need be (though Heaven forbid he should

suggest it himself) an alternative object of suspicion. He did wonder, though, why the august Merrick and the doughty Sohier seemed so pensive, so
terribly reserved as they prepared for the trial.
Husbanding their energies, no doubt.


Was it a good or bad sign that the jury was em-
panelled so swiftly? Bemis could hardly remember
a case of like importance when the swearing-in had
gone so smoothly. There had been sixty-one called,
the usual number of infirm, aged, out-of-state resi-
dents; another group (including one Samuel F.
Morse) challenged on the grounds of having already formed an opinion; and a new category altogether: those who asked to be excused for their
opposition to capital punishment. They could feel
confident that Chief Justice Shaw would not want
any jurymen whose judgement might be swayed
on account of some flabby disposition to leniency.
They were duly excused, though the bookseller
Benjamin Greene was insufficiently persuasive on
this score and was sworn anyway. With him were a
printer, a slater, two clerks, a painter, a dry goods
dealer, a merchant, an apothecary, a carpenter and
a furnisher plus the foreman, a locksmith, Robert
Byram. Together they were a group portrait of the
working trades of Boston; sweat-of-the-brow,
shirt-sleeve types with not a trace of the Brahmi-
nate in them.

For the duration of the trial, Clifford was lodging at the Tremont House, the stupendously grand hotel run by Dwight Boyden, who had trained the waiters in a precision drill that had become famous. All marched in step to the chiming of a bell: ONE take up positions behind chairs, TWO set down the silver, THREE serve the dishes, FOUR retreat into line, FIVE march smartly away. Bemis had gone to see him and found the Attorney General in his hotel slippers (provided while boots were being blacked) and had tried to persuade him to think of a substitute associate should his health fail. Clifford had looked at him incredulously (for he had not heard the ragged sound of Bemis's tubercular cough) and waved the idea away with a casual gesture of his white hand.

"No, no, what I'd like you to do, my dear Bemis, is to get up something of an opening for me. Don't trim it, mind, on my account, just write as you would for yourself."

And so he did, the two of them deciding on a deliberately spare recitation of the known facts of the case. The Government would establish, Mr. Clifford announced, first that Dr. Parkman had last been seen making his way to the College, second that the body parts discovered in the building were indeed those of the missing person. It would then proceed to show that the accused had a strong motive—namely, his debt—for the crime, and that his whole conduct when faced with its consequences gave the strongest possible impression of guilt.

Bemis listened, impressed. For all Clifford's habit of seeming laconic and mentally slack, he could, when the occasion called for it, become unexpectedly pithy. His normally rather monotonous, flat voice was paced, Bemis had to admit, to tremendous dramatic effect. Every time he said something as banal as "I am merely here to state a general outline" (of the evidence), the gallery hushed in expectation. When he followed this with "the bones found in the furnace, the parts found in the tea-chest and the parts found in the vault all constituted parts of one human body," there was an unstoppable outburst of exclamation and chattering that had Sheriff Eveleth shouting for silence. Clifford had the cunning, too, to avoid seeming persecutor rather than prosecutor. Should the prisoner be able to "give that explanation which shall carry conviction to your minds and to the minds of the entire civilised world and stand in the bright light of day . . . no one will have more gratification in the result than I shall."

He presented without qualification Bemis's own argument that if Webster were to be proved to have killed, it could not, being a voluntary act, be construed to be manslaughter rather than murder. It was a well-done opening, no doubt. Moreover, Clifford had declared publicly that he had wished his esteemed associate to offer the opening remarks but that he deferred to the learned opinions of others as to official proprieties (looking demurely at Justice Shaw). That was handsome of him. At least Bemis *thought* it was handsome of him, wasn't it?

After the Attorney General's address, the first witness appeared for the prosecution. Parkman's agent, Kingsley, recited for Bemis the circumstances of the disappearance, his part in the search of the College and his impression of Dr. Webster's behaviour after his arrest. Though he described the discovery of the body parts in detail that had the court in dead silence, he was not himself prepared to say that he recognised them as the Doctor's.

Sohier got up and languidly made his way to the witness stand. It had been unremarked just what Dr. Parkman's man was doing, acting the policeman all this time. Sohier reminded Kingsley of his part in twice searching Webster's house, once with no warrant, and of Webster's outrage at that, and got from him the admission that Dr. Parkman might use hard words if he felt crossed. The way it came out, though, was less than vindictive: "If a man had acted knavishly towards him he wouldn't hesitate to tell him so."

Bemis sat, arms crossed over his chest. Very good, he thought. Let the defence make the case for provocation. It will work to our purposes better than theirs.

## Accounts Rendered

In the afternoon Robert Gould Shaw testified, looking grim and frail. He too spoke of the disappearance, of the notices of reward. Unlike Kingsley, he did think the remains when he saw them were indeed those of his brother-in-law. Why? Because he had seen his hirsute form; once when told that he was too lightly dressed for the weather, Shaw said, Dr. Parkman had boasted of his hardiness by pulling up his pantaloons and showing he disdained even to wear drawers. Something about this intimacy, the sudden view, in the mind's eye, of white flesh and thick body hair, made the court-room stir. Backsides shifted uneasily on the benches; husbands took their wives' hands.

The following morning Marshal Tukey was first at the stand, looking crisp as fresh laundry. His answers were to the point, his manner, marshal-like; his expression during the few inconsequential questions of cross-examination, tolerant. Even those in the gallery who hated him, he knew, also admired him. And he got to produce the model, a marvellous miniaturisation of the Medical College in wood, complete with moveable walls, stairs and furnishings. One of the best doll-house makers in the city had done it for him. Such a pretty thing, heads craned to see it.

Still, the out-of-town reporters had hoped for more from the famous Tukey; something that would reveal the iron in the man beneath the Irish charm. And as the morning proceeded and the court heard from all the witnesses who said they had seen the Doctor near the College—the grocer Holland, the foundrymen, the young lads—they began to worry a bit and hear the impatient curses of their editors in Syracuse, Charleston, Cincinnati.

The doctors rescued them. The doctors would have the readers gaping. Thank God for the doctors. Following Coroner Pratt, five of them testified on that Wednesday afternoon. The first, Dr. Winslow Lewis, the chief of the post-mortem committee, brought with him a diagram illustrating the different sections of the body found in the furnace, the box and the privy vault. He set it on an easel and travelled over its details with his pointer, sometimes tapping against it for emphasis, sometimes leaning on the stick like a billiard player between breaks. Though forensic, his language was quite different from the severe monotonies of the law; it explored and reported from the anatomy unsentimentally but with a kind of sensuous exactness, a poetic attention to hue, that riveted the attention:

. . . posterior portion of integuments, from left scapula to right lumbar region, of a dark mahogany color and hardened . . . a little greenness under the right axilla (probably from commencing decomposition) and some blueness under the left axilla—leaving the skin soft, and easily broken. An opening slightly ragged, about one and a half inches in length under the left nipple.

When the inventory was done, the measurements of the separate pieces enumerated, he told George Bemis that nothing about them was dissimilar to what he might have expected to find in Dr. Parkman's body.

"But," asked Mr. Sohier with an extremely direct gaze at the witness, "had you not known he were missing, would you have said, right away, these are his mortal remains?"

"I would not."

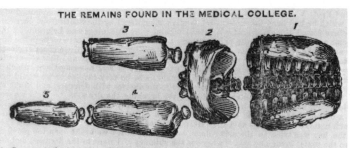

THE REMAINS FOUND IN THE MEDICAL COLLEGE.

o. 1.—Represents the vertebræ and thoracic cavity which is charred, and contains the lungs.
o. 2.—Represents the pelvic cavity, covered by flesh in its lower part.
o. 3.—The right thigh disarticulated from the pelvis.
o. 4.—The left thigh disarticulated from the pelvis.
o. 5.—The left leg disarticulated from the thigh and foot.

Neither could Dr. Stone, who followed, say he would *spontaneously* have thought these to be the mortal remains of Dr. Parkman had he not been looking for them, nor indeed could either man feel confident that the ragged hole in the left side of the sternum was indeed a stab wound of any kind.

Fine stuff, the reporters thought, good enough for the morning editions. But better was to follow in the person of Dr. Woodbridge Strong, physician and devotee of dissection. Winter was best, really, he explained, the low temperature kept the cadavers, of course; sometimes if the practice was slow he would go at it from eight in the morning to midnight. Oh dear, thought Bemis, even as he was preparing the next question. We have a singular man here. Look at him, red-faced, excessively jovial; the life and soul of the proceedings, a clown. Well, there he is and we had better proceed all the same.

Yes, yes, averred Dr. Woodbridge Strong, I know *all* about consuming corpses in fire. Why once in particular I recall Marshal Tukey (who some swore actually coloured at the invocation) giving me a pirate for dissection, and "it being warm weather I wanted to get rid of the flesh and only preserve the bones. He was a muscular stout man and I began upon it one night with a wood fire in a large old-fashioned fireplace. I built a rousing fire and sat up all night piling on wood and the flesh and got it consumed by morning."

Shall I stop him, thought Bemis? By Mr. Shaw's look of keen interest perhaps I had better not.

"I was afraid of a visit from the police, and by eleven o'clock they gave me a call, wanted to know what made such a smell in the street. I finished it up that forenoon. But I look upon it as no small operation, to burn up the body. It needs the right sort of fuel to begin with; wood *much* better than coal; pine kindlings, yes, ideal and you do need to stir it about now and then. You must have something the human flesh won't quench you see; always a difficult business on account of attracting suspicion by the smell. I have been called upon by my neighbors or the police several times on this account."

Yes, to be sure, thought Bemis, stealing a glance at Ned Sohier and taking stock of his expression of satisfaction. For no one had complained about any such smell in the College, had they? Indeed, only Littlefield's hand on the wall had suggested there was an active fire at all. At least his remarks about the wood had been helpful; all those grapevine pieces and kindling in the laboratory.

He was not finished yet. The blood? Oh, these pieces were extraordinary bloodless, "they seemed as much so as meat that is seen in the shambles." (A faint cry here from the upper gallery and a sudden scraping of a chair.) Justice Wilde looked ill, his face the colour of his silver hair; Chief Justice Shaw, even more interested, sat forward in his throne.

Good grief; enough, enough of this lunatic, thought Bemis, waving his hand in elaborate courtesy to Ned. Would he take his chances with him?

"Now Dr. Strong," Sohier began in that lovely drawl of his, "Dr. Strong, did you know Dr. Parkman well?"

"I visited him and had the pleasure of thinking he was one of my friends."

"But would you say you would know his naked body?"

"Oh I never saw any part of it though I should imagine his body hair was pretty much the same as on his head, gray that is and . . ."

He was off again. Bemis smirked behind his notes while trying to keep his eyes decently severe.

"I have made anatomy my special study for years you see and so I always examine most diligently the form of anyone I see. If I meet a man in the street whose shoulders are too much behind I notice it; if I meet a lady with a crook in her back I notice that too; what? No I would never try to burn a body in a *furnace* not at all right; the furnace in the College from which the slags were taken was, really a very poor thing to burn a body in."

It was too much; laughter finally broke, beginning in titters, suppressed as coughs; then little eruptions of soprano giggles; finally a great wave of shaking, roaring mirth sweeping over the public galleries, the press below, wrinkling the faces of

the clerks, the policemen, the counsels; even caus-
ing the odd twitch on the faces of the younger
Associate Justices. The Chief Justice, Bemis noticed, was stone-faced, staring directly with an
expression of contempt no less deep for being
impassive, at Webster, who was himself almost
doubled up in gales of hilarity.

It took a great deal of shouted commands, bang-
ing gavels and threats of clearances before the
dignity of the court-room was restored. Every so
often, at the recollection of the macabre bur-
lesque, a piggy snort or a deep, chortling heh-heh-
heh would escape like gas from a vent, before the
room was again sealed back up in solemnity and
embarrassment.

On the next day, the third of the trial, a Thursday,
the skies turned grey and a slicing easterly made
the crowds waiting outside the Court-house shiver
with the cold and wind their mufflers thick about
their faces. Yet there were more than the day
before, and so it would be until the very last hours.
When John Webster arrived, the usual hubbub
broke out; necks craned to see him smiling, shaking hands, occasionally clapping a hand about another's shoulder or back as if they, not he, needed
reassurance.

With the memory of Dr. Woodbridge Strong

mercifully dimmed, medical science could again appear in the witness stand with an aura of authority about it. Its next representative, though, was a man already marked by controversy: Charles Jackson, whose standing as an unimpeachable authority had suffered from the ether controversy. On this occasion he was simply asked to confirm his report to the Coroner, which stated that the remains had shown no traces of chemicals normally used to preserve bodies for dissection. There was then much talk of potash, acid, nitrate of copper, stains on the walls and alternative chemical means of reducing bodies. Attention wandered but was suddenly concentrated again when a knife was produced; its handle curved and intricately wrought, the gleaming blade six inches long. Jackson remembered it well; it had always been with Dr. Webster—on his desk in the old College, too—something to which he was obviously attached. When he had seen it after Dr. Parkman's disappearance he noticed—a good eye, Dr. Jackson—a slight film of oil on the blade, as though, perhaps, it had been cleaned?

Then the teeth appeared and with them Dr. Nathan Keep the dentist. A good town for dentists was Boston, with its partiality to taffy, stickjaw and puddings brimming with treacle. Dr. Keep, in his way, was a gentleman scholar, as erudite in his engagement in the tooth-and-jaw line as Dr. Strong was in the logistics of burning bodies. He

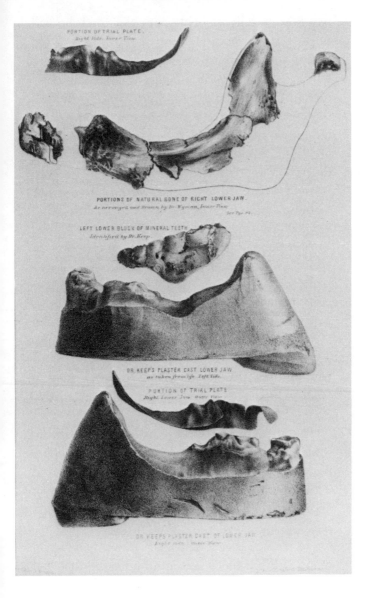

PORTION OF TRIAL PLATE.
*Right Side. Inner View.*

PORTIONS OF NATURAL BONE OF RIGHT LOWER JAW.
*As arranged and Drawn by Dr. Wyman, Inner View.*
*See Page 94.*

LEFT LOWER BLOCK OF MINERAL TEETH
*Identified by Dr. Keep.*

DR. KEEP'S PLASTER CAST LOWER JAW
*as taken from life. Left Side.*

PORTION OF TRIAL PLATE
*Right Lower Jaw. Outer View.*

DR. KEEP'S PLASTER CAST OF LOWER JAW
*Right Side. Outer View.*

was here to talk about the singular teeth he had made for Dr. Parkman, and if possible to avoid having to talk about his work for Dr. Webster's family. The latter were not happy clients; the girls' gums had been so dreadfully tortured, their Pa thought, and the dental fixings so unpleasantly temporary, that Dr. Keep had been dismissed altogether. The new dentist, clucking over what he diagnosed as a botched job, had to start over.

Not everyone, then, was in awe of Dr. Keep (nor would they be, even when he was appointed first Dean of the Harvard School of Dental Medicine). But for the moment, he was listened to with rapt attention, at least until from outside the Courthouse came the unmistakable sound of the fire-bells clanging. One of the police pushed his way urgently towards the Government table and told the Attorney General, to his horror, the Tremont House was on fire. "My papers, your Honour, my papers," was all he said, leaving George Bemis to ask for the adjournment readily granted.

The fire extinguished, the papers rescued from some pastry cook's neglect of an oven, the court reassembled; Dr. Keep had to begin again, and with more emotional labour than he had shown earlier. No one, he suggested, knew Dr. Parkman's peculiar jaw as well as he. Had he not been attending to it since 1822? When Dr. Lewis had shown him the fused block of teeth and bone that had been dug from the furnace, he knew right away he was looking at the Doctor's dentures.

The dentist's voice, which had begun with loud authority, had gradually lowered. Justice Metcalf had a hand cupped to his ear. Bemis was about to ask Dr. Keep to raise his tone when he realised the man was in tears. He attempted to go on; how . . . could he not . . . recognise it . . . when . . . It was no use. Bemis looked at the Chief Justice who (as far as one could tell) looked concerned. A few more sobs; a blow of the nose; and he went on.

The occasion was so exigent, Dr. Keep remembered, and the specifications so peculiar. The Doctor had particularly asked for them to be ready for the inauguration of the new College building (*his* building). But because of his extended nether jaw the whole had to be done in sections and connected to a gold plate by specially designed spiral springs. Without this little miracle of dental engineering, there was serious danger of teeth getting dislodged by the regular opening and closing of the mouth. It had been a close thing; accidents, breakings, ill fittings and even working through the very night before the opening of the new College, they were still not quite done. Dr. Noble, his assistant, just finished them not half an hour before the ceremony, so that the Dr. Parkman who left home that morning was turned into a quite different Dr. Parkman that evening; his smile became exceedingly white and even alarmingly brilliant. Even so, he was not quite happy for, he told Dr. Keep, his tongue seemed uncomfortably constricted for movement. Out came the plate; and in creating more space for the lower set, the grindwheel alas also took off the carefully shaded pink meant to represent the gums. Such pains, how could he ever forget such work?

The products of his art were passed around the court; the casts he had made of Parkman's jaws looked like miniature landscapes of outcrops and slopes and craters. Into one such declivity the Chief Justice gently placed the misshapen lump of mineral said to be teeth. It appeared to fit. There could be no mistake, Dr. Keep repeated, and what was more it was certain that for the fusion to show as it did, the head must have been put, whole, into the fire.

Pieces of Parkman were coming together. Then, with the next testimony, it seemed as though the Doctor himself had suddenly appeared in the room. On the easel before the court was a life-size drawing of a skeleton, shaded and tinted so that Dr. Jeffries Wyman could yet again identify the separated and recovered parts. Turned to left profile, it was apparent that this was not some generalised skeletal diagram. The protruding jaw, the long neck, all announced a very particular personality. As if it were not already vivid enough, he was shown with his arms swinging, the left leg extended backwards, toes pointing to the ground. It

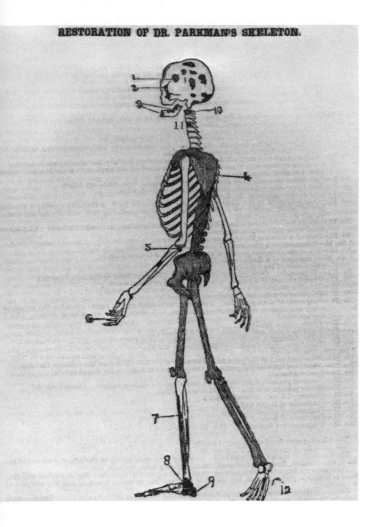

RESTORATION OF DR. PARKMAN'S SKELETON.

was the *Pedestrian* to the life; moving briskly towards the accused.

It was him they had all been waiting for; he knew it.
All those doctors and dentists and policemen. It
was his story they would listen to now. Oh, there
was some as hated him and looked down at him, he
knew that; he was accusing a Professor wasn't he,
one of the old sort too and one the world knew had
called him a villain. He'd heard about it, the signs at
Dr. Parkman's funeral calling him a liar and a
rogue. Someone had even told him as how he's
been written about in those New York papers as
"low and contemptible" or some such. Well, they
would have to listen to him now wouldn't they?

"I have no middle name" was the first thing
Ephraim Littlefield told the court. He said it in a
bold, clear tone as if defying rebuke, bragging his
plainness. His place, he told the plain men of the
town—the locksmith and the printer and the dry
goods man who sat on the jury—was among the
common sort, the sort whose mothers (if they
knew them) had no business sticking their own
names between a first and last. He was what he
was. He had no middle name.

So then, brought along by George Bemis, he
told his story: the overheard arguments between
Parkman and Webster; his growing suspicions after the disappearance; the slackness of the police

searches; his own determination to break into the
privy vault from below; and his terrible journey
through dust and darkness to revelation. He was,
thought the attorney, a born storyteller. To be sure,
he had practised this enough: to Marshal Tukey,
Coroner Pratt, the Grand Jury and again to
Clifford and himself. Still, Bemis sensed in the
janitor a teller of tales; more in the way of an old
sailor than a fairground yarn-spinner, but a man
who had a way with an audience nonetheless; one
who knew how to set a scene: four candles burning
in Dr. Webster's back room, and he with his nose in
a chemistry volume as the irate Parkman marched
in.

All through Friday morning, with just a break of
a quarter of an hour, Littlefield went on; reporters
scribbled frantically as macabre detail piled on
detail. "Professor Webster sent for me to buy a
piece of lime as big as my head," he finished before
the adjournment was called. In the afternoon one
pressman measured the excitement caused by Littlefield's testimony by the number of aged sep-
tuagenarian gentlemen, "some with specs on their
nose; some with bald heads and others with their
silvery locks," who notwithstanding the foul air
and the dangerous press of persons, felt they had to
be present at such a moment.

Aware that this was the most powerful act of the
drama, the Attorney General took over the questioning. When the time came for Littlefield to

relate the moment he looked through the brick hole and saw what lay on the earth, John Clifford came closer to the stand and in absolute quiet asked, "What was your condition when you came up out of the cellar?"

Pliny Merrick jumped up to object that that was hardly to the point in anything concerning Dr. Webster and was duly overruled.

Littlefield replied, simply: "I was very much affected."

It was Saturday morning before the defence got to their cross-examination. By now, Sheriff Eveleth had entirely given up trying to instruct the huge crowd that battled its way into the courtroom and galleries as to where they should sit. Even counting heads, with this immense number, was absurd. So the police merely waited until every conceivable space—steps, passages, chairs, benches, column pedestals—was full before pressing the doors shut against even more people trying to force an entry. The Sheriff had never seen anything like it, not for old Lafayette in 1825, not even for Fanny Kemble.

What was it that had magnetised them all? The play of death and retribution? The faintly disgusting excitement to be had from observing a man of the learned, moneyed classes revealed as a murdering beast? This very morning the circus awaited a gladiator act: the nimble, sophisticated Mr. Sohier waiting with trident and net to ensnare the stubby broadsword of Ephraim Littlefield. Some sort of fall surely was guaranteed.

To general amazement (not least George Bemis's) it failed to happen. Ned Sohier picked and pecked at Littlefield's testimony, at the soundness of his memory, without ever inflicting a fatal wound on his credibility. Instead of Littlefield's slips of the tongue working against him, they produced the kind of hearty laughter that trivialised the counsel's attack. Did he not have a *particular* place for the broom that swept the stove ashes on the twenty-third?

"No it was left everywhere" (meaning anywhere). Howls of laughter.

Then the turkey returned, or rather Littlefield's change of mind about exactly when Webster had given the order for it. He had told the Grand Jury it was Wednesday and now recalled it was Tuesday. The line of questioning was not a quibble, for had Webster offered the gift before the most thorough police search, the sinister implication that it was given for some sort of collusion might be lost. But it was Littlefield's casual way with recall that the counsel was after and Sohier succeeded in muddling him further. Yet somehow in his taciturn retreat there was an impression of unapologetic honesty:

"I can't say . . . it was a mistake."

"How came you to get Wednesday and Tuesday so confused together in your mind?"

"Can't say."

Although the court-room began to be bemused by all these Tuesdays and Wednesdays and turkeys before and turkeys after and to wonder what in Heaven's name it had to do with murder, Bemis and Clifford saw very well what the defence was up to. Not only Littlefield's memory had to be shown to be faulty. He had also to be revealed as a shifty, obsessively suspicious, prying, snooping fellow bent from the beginning on the Professor's destruction. Many questions, then, were taken up with the day and time at which his suspicions spurred him to action, even when there seemed little base for them. But the janitor's obtuseness here again helped him out. He was ready to admit that he had his feelings as early as Sunday, especially when Dr. Webster came up to tell him about paying the Doctor off. Well, he glared back at Sohier, so if it were a feeling; an' weren't it a right one then?

John Webster's great wad of notes for Merrick and Sohier had insisted that Littlefield be shown as a dangerous, greedy, immoral rogue; who traded in dead bodies; who in all likelihood had dug them fresh from the grave; who had bloodied his hands in chopping and tearing. But, to Webster's mounting consternation, as Littlefield's clipped, direct, unvarnished answers fell one by one into the room, neither Merrick nor Sohier did anything of the sort. Oh, he was asked if it was true that he was a gambler, that he had played cards the very night of Dr. Parkman's disappearance and that the Doctor had discovered him. But when he declined to answer that, no one on the bench required him to do so. That he readily acknowledged that he was dancing through the same week that he listened through door cracks, climbed through windows, burrowed below the building like a mole—what did this do except make him more of a regular fellow? After the Monday search he was off to Bryant's Dancing Academy; on Wednesday to a cotillion party; on Thanksgiving to the Sons of Temperance Ball. What was so wrong with that? Plain, no-middle-name Ephraim Littlefield: the terpsichorean sleuth.

When the cross-examination had finished, it was clear to everyone in the room that its intended victim was still on his feet, his broadsword in hand. The janitor had beaten off the gentleman, and not by the sharpness, but by the bluntness, of his wits. By making himself no angel he had avoided being shown as a devil. He was just a working-man who played cards where he shouldn't and was immoderately fond of the cotillion. But he knew what he knew and had the boldness to act on it.

And there was one vice he wouldn't have set on him neither. The Attorney General helped him out here, asking, at the very end, whether he had ever mentioned to anyone at all (as Webster had said) that he might seek a reward?

"I never have made, or intended to make, any claim for either of the rewards which have been offered. I have so declared and now state that I disavow all claim henceforth."

The profession was greeted by only a few gasps of disbelief. Bemis thought: "Never underestimate this man; a canny fellow; he is after bigger things."

The imprudent boy inside George Bemis exulted "the thing is done; the case is won." But the wise attorney cautioned wariness: "Come, your own arguments are not yet even complete; the defence has not even begun its own." The Transcendentalist ("what does any of it matter anyway?") was on leave for the duration of the trial. But, taking supper with his father that Saturday night and trying to anoint his hacking lungs with port (as though digestion could ease respiration), he found it difficult to be pessimistic.

What truly gave him pause was the foggy and feeble cross-examination of his witnesses. It was already evident that Pliny Merrick was an elegantly dressed nonentity who should have kept his title of Judge to impress the railroad directors. But what had happened to Ned Sohier? It was he, after all, who was manifestly the true designer of the defence and he who had seemed so excessively delicate as its executor. Watching him go at Littlefield was like seeing a man attack a brick wall with a fencing foil: the weapon was altogether too subtle for the job.

Without particularly meaning to, Mrs. Littlefield had helped a great deal. Her testimony, coming directly after her husband's, had supplied an affecting scene of domesticity thrown into horrified turmoil by her husband's discovery; of small children being shunted about those gloomy corridors; of doors closing "for I did not wish to hear or know anything more about the matter."

The case had gone far. With the help of the weeping dentist and his plates, the prosecution had shown that the body in question had surely once been George Parkman. And Littlefield's story had been bold enough to carry conviction. It now remained to show the documents that would supply the motive and bring to court all those who had witnessed John Webster's reaction when confronted with the remains. So instead of the slightly rumpled, bespectacled professor, the jury would be given a picture of a man in the extremity of guilty torment. After all, it was an article of faith for them all, be they Catholic or Congregationalist, Spiritualist or Sabbatarian: guilt will write itself on the face and the body; the mark of Cain would erupt beneath even the most unblemished skin. Men who had seen Macready's *Macbeth* said there was nothing like it.

It proceeded according to plan. On Monday the policemen told their story of discovery and arrest, of burned bones and trembling hands. Derastus Clapp appeared and spoke, for the first time, of the money; of searching the house at Garden Street. Mrs. Webster had produced a bundle of the Professor's papers, among which were two notes, one the old Parkman loan of 1842; the second the joint loan of 1847. A third "memorandum" full of additions and subtractions made clear what part of that second loan was due to Dr. Parkman and how he declined to surrender the note until it was fully paid. So, had Dr. Webster not paid it from his lecture tickets? A cashier of the Charles River Bank declared that on November 23, Professor Webster's account was still overdrawn, since he had used his ticket money to pay rent and other bills.

Family members appeared: the Reverend Francis Parkman, looking more than usually gaunt, described John Webster's visit on the Sunday as disconcertingly like "a business visit." Samuel Parkman Blake, who had come to see Dr. Webster on the Monday after the disappearance, said, "His stiffness of manner seemed as though he did not anticipate a visit from me. He said very little about the search and made no enquiries about the family." What he did do, though, was to tell Blake about a recent visitation from George who, after a lecture, had gone straight up to him and said, "Doctor, I want some money; you have five hundred dollars in your wallet and I want it." "The countenance of Doctor Webster positively lit up when he told me this," said Blake, looking at the bench.

On Tuesday evening, near seven o'clock, as energies were flagging and Justice Shaw's appetite was calling for supper service, Marshal Tukey was brought to the stand a second time. When he was shown three letters, he confirmed they had been written to him during the week after the disappearance. At which point Mr. Clifford rose and told the court the Government's evidence was really complete, except for a proof, to be shown, that all these letters were, in fact, written by the prisoner.

What did they say, these letters? One had an air of helpfulness about it:

Dear Sir: You will find Dr. Parkman murdered on Brooklyn Heights.
 Yours truly M—Captain of the Dart

Another was a kind of thick scrawl, almost painted rather than written:

Dr. Parkman was took on bord herculan and this al I dare to say or I shal be kiled—Est Cmbrge—one of the men give me his watch but I was feared to keep it and thod it in the water right side the road to the long bridge to Boston.

A third, signed "Civis," was elaborately public-spirited, affecting a rather learned manner:

Mr. Tukey, Dear Sir: I have been considerably interested in the recent affair of Dr. Parkman and I think I can recommend means, the adoption of which might result in bringing to light some of the mysteries. . . .

Had outhouse floors been raked carefully in the search? Had cellars been attended to?

Probably his body was cut up and placed in a stout bag and thrown off one of the bridges—perhaps Craigie's—and I would recommend the firing of cannon from some of these bridges and from various parts of the harbor in order to cause the body to rise to the surface of the water.

Yours respectfully,

And so, on Tuesday morning, the experts were brought on. Boston loved experts. It had already heard from experts on teeth, bones, body-burning, eavesdropping. In the press it had heard from mesmerists, phrenologists, physiognomists, Spiritualists and those who believed the source of the human personality lay deep in the serpentine intestines. Why not, then, a handwriting expert?

Asked whether the letters were, in fact, written by Dr. Webster, the expert, one Nathaniel Gould, was about to give his answer when Sohier objected, and loudly too. Yes, he knew that such evidence had been admitted in *Moody* v. *Rowell,* but it was warranted only when a genuine specimen of handwriting was compared with another said to be by the accused. In this case, there could be no question that any of these letters were written in anything remotely approximating Dr. Webster's hand. Ah, came back Clifford, we propose to show precisely that they are in his "handwriting" if by that we take all the variations and alterations possible in a hand.

The argument, batted to and fro, was settled by the Chief Justice, who allowed the evidence on the grounds that disguised hands had been allowed in cases of arson, blackmail and the like. Expert Gould then took as his base text Dr. Webster's notes and jottings on the loan notes—things dashed off rather than formally written—and then compared them with the three letters; *d*'s "peculiarly turned at the end of words," *R*'s made without a hook; closed *a*'s.

But there was a word, which if truly written in John Webster's hand as Expert Gould insisted, was more damning than all these letters set together. That word had been marked on the face of one of George Parkman's notes. It said "Paid."

The case for the Government had taken more than a week. The case for the defence would take barely more than two days. Was it so bereft of persuasion? After hearing the story—which no one in

Boston would ever forget in his lifetime—related in so many ways, in so many narratives whose tracks crossed and recrossed, deviated and turned back on themselves but which, finally, came together in one broad highway, how could an alternative path to the truth be established? Yet, somehow that had to be done. The defence had to produce a version of this history that was as compelling, as moving, as vivid and as persuasive as the one the court had heard told and retold. The defence had shown no taste for fisticuffs when put up against the likes of Derastus Clapp or Ephraim Littlefield. But at the very least Sohier had to turn storyteller.

George Bemis watched him with sympathy and with a trace of condescension as he began. Just a few minutes into Sohier's speech it was apparent that sympathy was out of place. For here was Ned Sohier—looking much older than his forty-odd years, with his grey whiskers and bald head—the image of the Yankee Uncle in his cheerful vest, unexpectedly turned dramatist, acting the pants off everyone else in the court.

Was it only a minute or two before he invoked, without a name, that institution whose honour and virtue were really on trial, the college that was "one of the boasts of our city . . . where numbers now present including myself were educated, where memory whose very form and features are associated with pleasant recollections"?

And after Mother Harvard came family, the domestic nest.

Gentlemen, is the life of Professor Webster forfeited to the laws of this country because it has been proved here, beyond all reasonable doubt, that he has committed one of the most horrible offences which can be enumerated even on the law's dark catalogue of crime? Upon you it devolves to say whether Professor Webster shall go hence to his family and there remain what he has ever been to them the very centre of their purest and holiest affection, the very object of their idolatry, or whether he shall go hence to the scaffold. . . . Yes, gentlemen, it devolves upon you to say whether the fire upon his hearth stone shall henceforth burn brightly and be cast on happy faces beaming kindly upon him, or whether your breath, Mr. Foreman, when you pronounce the verdict shall extinguish that fire scattering its ashes to the winds. . . . If you err you see the victim. He it is and his family who must be offered up as a sacrifice to that error unless indeed you err on mercy's side. There you may err and err in safety and no prisoner's groan, no widow's sob, no orphan's tear bear witness to your error.

So, he went on, the jury owed it to the family to eradicate from their minds the slightest shadow of bias and prejudice they may have earlier formed, in order to allow Professor Webster a true and full defence.

Then followed two further disquisitions, the first on "prejudice"; the second on the distinction between manslaughter and wilful murder, delivered in silvery, beautiful elocution. Bemis was lost in admiration; Clifford's bored expression quite failed to disguise his anxiety. First:

Prejudice is blind; it is contagious; it is communicated by the eye and in speaking here between man and man I do not pretend to say that there is any man in your panel untainted by prejudice. By no means are we to forget, Gentlemen, or are we to suppose, that you have forgotten, the great excitement which existed in this city when it was first bruited abroad that George Parkman was murdered? Do we now forget that men quit their avocations—that they were clustered together in corners, in the doors, in stores, houses and churches—and that their conversation was upon this one point and on no other. Have we forgotten the great indignation that was excited in this community—so creditable to the community but so dangerous to the defendant—when it was first announced that the body was found in the Medical College in his laboratory? Have we forgotten the prejudices against Professor Webster? Have we forgotten these things? By no means! They are burned into our memories.

If such prejudices are truly set aside, the behaviour of the defendant after his arrest looks quite different from the construction put upon it by the police and the prosecution. "Consider, I say, how we proceed. We seize upon a man, tear him from his family and while his mind is paralysed by the very idea and crime imputed to him, by the danger of his situation and by the grief and despair of his family we tell him to prepare for his defense. What next? Why *ex parte* proceedings go on. The matter is heard and adjudicated by a coroner's jury where he is not present. It is afterward tried by a grand jury where he is not represented.

"And now," said Sohier, appearing somehow to rise with indignation several inches above his usual height, "now he is brought to trial after a mass of opinion launched against him and *here too* he is denied the possibility of speaking on his own behalf." He looked steadily at the bench. Such practises as barring a defendant from taking the stand on grounds of potential self-incrimination were, he thought, the rankest hypocrisy. No wonder he practised civil law in this state.

Second disquisition. The jury should understand that murder is killing with malice aforethought; either "express malice" of the kind wherein a man lies in wait for another; or even, under the law, "malice implied," wherein a man kills through a dangerous and wicked disposition. Manslaughter, on the other hand, "committed in the heat of blood" with provocation, was not legally held to be "a cruel act." The difference between murder from malice *implied,* then, and manslaughter was a fine line, but across it lay the issue of life or death for the defendant.

At this point, Bemis noticed, Clifford seemed noticeably more relaxed, and he knew why. For all the elegance of Sohier's diction, the drama of his oratory, he had suddenly, needlessly fallen into a pit of his own making and he surely would not clamber out again. Even to introduce, in the opening speech, the distinction between man-slaughter and murder, and to make a law-school lecture out of it, was in effect to concede that there had indeed been a homicide. Yet the rest of the defence's case attacked the Government's assumption that Dr. Parkman had indeed met his end in Webster's rooms at the College on November 23. They could *either* try to chisel away at the connecting evidence that supplied this assumption *or* they could concede that it had happened but that it had been an unpremeditated, provoked manslaughter. And "alternative defences" had not been un-known. But he could not seriously expect the jury to credit, at the same time, two mutually contradictory histories.

Did Sohier not see this as he went on? It seemed not, or perhaps he hoped his eloquence would mask the glaring inconsistency. For the time being he concentrated on arguing that the Government needed to show, beyond *all* doubt, exactly how and in what manner Dr. Parkman had died and that the Grand Jury indictment, in including every conceiv-

able manner of attack (stabbing, kicking, wound-
ing, bruising and even "by manner unknown") was
itself an absurdity. Here the English Common Law
tradition provided for such portmanteau indict-
ments but Sohier was able to make sport with this.
If actually executed in such a fashion, he implied,
the victim would be double- and treble-dead.
What was more, he went on, since the Government's case rests so critically on the assumption
that Dr. Parkman never came out from the Medical College, what if the defence could produce
witnesses who would swear the contrary? "Now I
will show that if we break one link of their chain we
break all."

But as soon as Sohier announced his concentra-
tion on strategy number one, he immediately
switched to strategy number two. Twenty-three
witnesses were called, including President Sparks,
colleagues at Harvard, neighbours like Judge Fay
and the whist-devotees, the Treadwells, all of
whom confirmed, more or less, that while occasionally given to irritability, Dr. Webster was the
very milk of human kindness.

There were, however, three more persons who
could attest his innocence better than any other,
for they had never for one minute thought otherwise. Marianne, Harriet and Catherine Webster
brought to the court the light of 22 Garden Street,
not the darkness of the Medical College. Marianne
and her sisters spoke of tea and gardening, card

games and poetry readings. They were, indeed, as the clichés of the newspaper reporters had it, "lovely," with the grace of young women about them but shining with the challenged loyalty of children. They stood in dark high-necked dresses like novice nuns put to the test. With dark eyes set in a white face, Marianne appeared resolved to master her sorrow, to defy calumny; Harriet, the fifteen-year-old, clutched a handkerchief for strength; Catherine, the youngest, was so scared and disturbed that her voice would barely rise above a velvety whisper. Bemis had no intention of sullying the poignancy of the moment with a searching cross-examination. To what end? He suddenly noticed Dr. Webster trembling in his chair, his face buried in both hands. He nodded to the Sheriff to have a regard to this, but when Catherine left the stand Dr. Webster seemed to recover his composure, though his face was creased and tight, as though attacked by a violent headache.

Medical men followed; the defence's medical men, some of whom—Dean Holmes, Dr. Lewis, Dr. Gay—had also been the prosecution's medical men. But with the commendable impartiality of their calling, carefully led by Sohier, they now proceeded to emphasise the difficulty, from pathological evidence alone, of determining at all in what manner the body had met its end.

Still more dramatic was the appearance of William Morton, Boston's most famous dentist, the man who had been the first in history to administer anaesthetic for surgery. He took a directly opposite view to Dr. Keep's on the matter of dental recognition. For all statements otherwise he saw nothing at all so peculiar in the plate, or the ground cast, to help any sort of identification of the fused teeth. Take the extension of Dr. Parkman's lower jaw, for example, all dentists have many such cases among their clients. How are we to know it was this particular one? Bemis pressed a cross-examination; Chief Justice Shaw joined in. Are we really to say that Dr. Parkman's jaw was not peculiar? Of course it was, Dr. Morton replied with quiet determination, but not so that another's plate might not actually fit him, for all the peculiarities.

Riding high on this wave of organised scepticism, following the midday dinner adjournment, Sohier called a parade of seven witnesses, all of whom swore they had in fact seen Dr. Parkman in the afternoon of the twenty-third, when, according to the prosecution, he was already lying dead inside the College. They were all unequivocal about their recollection. William Thompson, the clerk at the East Cambridge Registry of Deeds, was the same man who had gone to see Webster at his house on the twenty-fifth to check the date of the mortgage on his mineral collection. He re-

membered seeing the Doctor that Friday particularly for he had just got himself a new coat that
afternoon; the one he now had on, in fact.

Bemis tried to shake him. He was a clerk, spent
his days copying. How was his sight? Didn't he use
spectacles?

"Never."

"A magnifying glass."

"Not habitually, just to examine very fine
writing."

"Have you never told anyone you could write
finely in the mesmeric state?"

"No, Sir, I never use the term *mesmeric*. I may
have said something about the *biological* state. I
sometimes lecture in biology."

Everyone around here loves to lecture, Bemis
thought.

"Well, what have you said about writing in the
biological state?"

"I may have told Mr. Andrews, your informant, I
could write in a very fine hand in the biological
state. I never told him I could write so finely I
could not read it in my natural state. No I do not
pretend I can see better in the biological state than
the natural." And unspoken, written on his face: "I
am the clerk of the Registry of Deeds; do not you
make me out a poor deluded person."

The others, Mrs. Philena Hatch, Mrs. Abby
Rhoades and her daughter, were quite as determined. So the Attorney General proposed, in re-

buttal, to call a group of witnesses all of whom had *thought* they had seen Dr. Parkman but on speaking to the person, discovered they were mistaken. The defence objected, angrily. A conference proceeded on the bench and for the first time in the trial the objection was allowed; the evidence was declined.

Well, it shan't hurt us much, Bemis told himself, for look where the defence have placed themselves. They must now proceed on this path of confusion and uncertainty. To be sure, the law bids them to do so since murder may only be proved beyond all reasonable doubt. But juries, he knew, these good ordinary men, do not wish to be confused; the precise instinct of the locksmith and the printer, the accounting of the clerk and the dry goods merchant, all rebel against it. Give them an *alternative* story they can superimpose over the histories of Ephraim Littlefield and Derastus Clapp and they perhaps may prefer it. But give them only uncertainty and they will squirm with unhappiness like children sent to bed without their story's end.

From the outset of Pliny Merrick's closing address, it appeared that this was indeed to be the defence's strategy. It took a little while for this to become quite plain because the senior counsel (unlike his associate) spoke in elaborately turned phrases, in long sentences whose main clauses appeared only gradually like mountains emerging from the mist. It was as though he were addressing the jury in German, and a cultivated High German at that.

Yet what he said, when he said it, was telling. The Government had to prove three things, all essential for its case: that George Parkman was dead and dead from "the agency of another person," that the prisoner at the bar was that person *and* that he committed the homicide with malice aforethought. The Government has taken an "unusual" time to do this. Why? Because their case must be made by deductions from a great many collateral facts; their evidence is "indirect, presumptive, circumstantial."

Suppose, he went on, as many witnesses (whose credibility he proceeded at length to insist was unimpeachable) have testified, Dr. Parkman *did* leave the College and was seen about town. Since there is no evidence whatsoever he saw Dr. Webster subsequent to their meeting, the case must fall away. Indeed, contrast their certainty with the kind of evidence the Government has produced: "mangled remains." True, he admitted "it would be difficult to assign any satisfactory reason why they should not be regarded as parts of one and the same body. Still it is a question upon which your judgement must be passed."

More responsibilities for the jury!

Was it truly Dr. Parkman? Dr. Keep recognised his teeth, but Dr. Morton refuted any dentist's ability to do so with teeth in such a state of damage. Who is right? Who shall say? There must at least be a serious doubt as to the proof. Likewise, amidst all the evidence of rending here and holes and punctures there, no one can confidently say in which *exact* manner this person died or was killed.

Bemis looked at the jury. The foreman looked troubled, frowning; others sat in deep stillness; one or two with their chins resting in their hands. Were they merely exhausted (as he certainly was), or were they wavering? After all these years, he still never quite knew how to read a jury's mind. It was as if they had departed from their individual wills and were now gathered together under a shroud of shared pensiveness.

And then, without warning, logic or, it seemed to Bemis, any sense, Pliny Merrick swerved his carriage. "By God he's doing it," Bemis rejoiced, even before the fatal words dropped from Merrick's lips.

"Gentlemen of the Jury, I must now pass to the consideration of other and different subjects. Should all the objections which I have made be overcome and should you arrive at the conclusion that it is proved beyond reasonable doubt that Dr. Parkman was killed by some human agent, it becomes essential to ascertain what was the crime which was committed by the person who was guilty of the homicide.

"In considering this question, I must for the

present assume that the homicide was committed by the prisoner at the bar and I must assume also for the purposes of this examination the existence and the truth of the various facts of which the Government have supplied you with evidence."

"Assume," such a little, little word, Bemis thought. For gentlemen such as him and me and all the Harvard classmates sitting in this room, it signifies something hypothetical, suppositious, intellectually experimental. But, my learned friend and fool, you have *assumed* too much; you have used it to those good tradesmen and mechanics over there. They are more accustomed to hearing it mean "take for granted" as in "we may assume you owe me twenty dollars for these groceries."

From an unexpected shifting of persons and furniture (and perhaps from Ned Sohier's transparently stricken expression), Merrick suddenly realised his blunder. "I earnestly desire you not to misunderstand . . . any erroneous concessions of Professor Webster. You will understand, distinctly, that he denies all participation in the homicide of Dr. Parkman, that he pleads not guilty." Yet he went on—should, alas, you conclude he nonetheless did so, it is for the Government to show why the charge should not be manslaughter.

Quicksand. Bemis had seen it once on the shore of Cape Anne; had thrown a long black stick that slid below the sucking circle and was gone. He imagined Merrick, a long, black, impeccably attired stick, with the sand beneath him very slowly taking his boots, his pants, his watch fob, with him all the time continuing the grandiloquent diction of his address.

It got better. At the end of the morning, he conceded there was no way to prove where Webster got the money to pay off Dr. Parkman's note. Not, you understand, that he had not done so from a little savings here and there, but only that it could not be proved.

It got still better in the afternoon. For when, at last, Merrick turned narrator, the story he related (and did so pretty well), was one which set yet again in the jury's mind the indelible image of a distracted, prodigal man attacking his creditor. It was, he said, a tale of passion, and

it is impossible to know how men will conduct themselves under the domination of passion in its highest excitement. Professor Webster occupied an important position—was a man of good standing in society. He had a wife and daughters dependent upon his professional labors and ability; he was poor, and all before him might look like ruin and desolation. While his blood was hot and his passion high and his victim just slain, suppose that he commits just one rash act more. There, surrounded as he was by walls which excluded the presence of all witnesses and shut out all human observation the temptation might come upon him to conceal; and the mutilation of the body would mark the first act of concealment.

Bemis thought: Well, you have surely convinced me, my friend. He now envied Clifford the opportunity of the closing.

Clifford thought: I know why he's doing this. He doesn't believe Webster. He knows he did it but he can't stand to see him hanged.

Franklin Dexter, sitting near the front of the court, thought: Dear God, Choate was right; we can't say, at once, he didn't do it but if he did it ain't murder.

Rufus Choate, sitting one row behind, thought: How on earth did this man ever get to be a judge, even in the Court of Common Pleas?

When Merrick reverted again to exposing the circumstantiality of the Government's evidence, by emphasising the bloodless and spotless nature of Webster's laboratory and by noting the fact that the stains on the wall were nitric acid not blood, it all seemed a prolonged (exceedingly prolonged, thought the Justices) footnote to a famous debacle.

It was getting dark before Merrick finally got around to challenging the credibility of Littlefield's testimony. But he hardly did so in the terms that John Webster had obligingly set before him. There was no talk of a "resurrection man," a doubtfully reformed drunk; no "we do not attempt to impeach the general character of Mr. Littlefield for truth and veracity." (More fool you, muttered Bemis.) "Some mistakes he has made; some errors he has fallen into . . . but upon these matters I am not disposed to dwell."

What then? Only that it was very peculiar that because he had formed so deep and so early a suspicion of Dr. Webster, he did not do *more* about it in the way of telling the police. Was it not odd that it was only after a reward had been offered that he got to it in earnest? At last, however, Merrick got to the point: that it was even odder that the janitor had done his tunnelling and battering against the wall entirely of his own accord and without any help. Could it be that this was because he knew, in advance, what he might find? How strange that he knew so precisely where to break through the wall.

If the effect of these "perplexities" in his story "is to implicate him in any connection whatever with these remains before the breach was made . . . then you must not place any reliance on his testimony. And if through the loss of this testimony the great chain of circumstantial evidence which presses upon the prisoner's life is interrupted or broken the whole mass of network, the great theories and hypotheses of the Government will give way and disappear as the cloud and mist are dispersed by the beams of the rising and refreshing sun."

But it would not stick. Compared with the gripping tale of money and *passion,* the effort to implicate Littlefield—to tell a rival story—was tentative and pallid. No one would remember it, much less believe it, when the time came for the jury to be closeted.

So there were doubts; so some, perhaps much, of the evidence was circumstantial. And so, as Merrick finished by emphasising, the Professor's character had been exemplary; that of a devoted, affectionate family man. Ought his utter helpless terror when locked up and confronted with a charge of murder be taken as an admission of guilt? Remember, he said, that in every case of doubt, good reputation shall deliver the accused.

God grant him, in this day of peril, a good deliverance; and (looking at the jury) may he grant it to you also, that you may never reflect upon your final determination here but with inward peace and satisfaction — a peace that shall sustain you in life and be to you a crown of joy in death.

A rum peroration, thought Bemis — half Sunday sermon, half melodrama. Will those sturdy jurymen really be happy to be told to consider their own end?

The eleventh and last day, a Saturday. The sky had gone pasty, the hue of clotted cream on the turn. By the time the Court-house opened, fat, sluggish flakes of snow had begun to drop. It was that most trying season in Boston: hopes of spring, of the green resurrection of the earth, were deadened by the obstinate grip of winter. In John Webster's back yard in Garden Street, crocus and scylla were quickly covered by the silent white sheet.

Clifford rose, delivered superbly backhanded compliments to the eloquence, the grace, the *ingenuity,* the *resourcefulness* of his learned colleagues for the defence. He had hoped, though, as he had said at the outset of the proceedings, that some sort of explanation would be forthcoming as to the "terrible circumstances that had woven a web around him which now seems to be irresistibly contracting to its doom. I grieve to say to you after all that has been done and said, that hope is utterly disappointed."

Circumstantial evidence? Yes, but what of it. "So, strictly speaking, is almost all evidence." How many murderers should ever be punished if the case had to hang on direct eyewitnesses alone? "The law exacts a conviction wherever there is *legal* evidence to show the prisoner's guilt beyond a reasonable doubt and circumstantial evidence is legal evidence." Suppose, for example, that four professors had seen Dr. Parkman go into the laboratory and not come out, had entered and found his clothes and property there but no body? Suppose further that Dr. Webster had said "I have murdered Dr. Parkman" but subsequently recanted? Would this mean there was no case? Even if the jury is in doubt as to whether Dr. Parkman died by knife or a hammer blow, if they are but satisfied that it was Dr. Webster who committed the deed, "no matter how he did it, he cannot escape the violated justice of this Commonwealth."

As for the remains, could anyone who had paid attention to Dr. Wyman's drawing doubt that the remains were Dr. Parkman's? Is it to be supposed that the funeral and the solemn interment were a cruelly bungled mistake? That someone else's remains are buried beneath Trinity Church? As for those who imagined they saw Dr. Parkman in the afternoon, like the *biological* witness Mr. Thompson, doubtless they saw someone very like the Doctor. But had it truly been he, surely not six but six hundred or six thousand would have come forward to attest it. Was he not the great *Pedestrian*?

Bemis listened to Clifford carefully. It was quite a technique, he had to concede; more than he had ever imagined from the rather morose, put-upon man eating his supper at the Tremont: a shrewd mixture of the pious and the ironic. I wager, if this turns out well, he will go into politics and go far, too.

What followed was even better: the melodrama of the Sacred Teeth. Dr. Keep and his "long and patient labor" in producing the dentures in time for the inauguration were invoked. When Clifford

considered that it was on those very premises that
Dr. Parkman met his fate and the marks of his
identity were discovered, he seemed "to see in it
the guiding hand of Almighty God, leading us to
the discovery of the truth." There followed even
more sublime threnodies on the holy cause of science vilely debased by the prisoner. To the minis-
ters of the healing arts, all respect and honour were
due for so serving the cause of justice and truth.
"When we have welcomed them to our bedsides,
amid our trials and sufferings, we have loved and
honoured them; but when we do meet them here
and see them taking the stand—as they do most
reluctantly against one of their own brotherhood,
. . . giving themselves unreservedly to the truth, let
it strike where it may . . . they have my humble
reverence."

And so it went on. The defence had played on
the strings of virtue, on character, on reputation.
Very well, evidence aside, they shall be outplayed
in that key.

What Clifford then proceeded to do, Bemis
thought, exhibited skills of high theatrical quality.
One day, he predicted, actors will mimic his and
my rhetoric; we shall have Littlefields in grease-
paint and Websters in sham eyeglasses. But whoever tries to capture John Clifford will not, as it
might be said, do him justice.

Littlefield had been cast in a sinister light; then
let him be recast again as the very incarnation of

simple virtue. Webster's reputation, his standing, his outward propriety had been invoked on his behalf; very well, let it count against him. So the Attorney General from New Bedford did something guaranteed to win him applause in Boston: he set the character of a working-man against the pretensions of the Cambridge professorate. To Littlefield "and to his wife and children, his reputation is as dear as that of a college professor is to him and in the eye of the law is entitled to equal consideration." Has he not had to endure gross libel, unsupported imputations; has he not gone through the ordeal of intense cross-examination? And yet, "he has come out of that fiery furnace . . . without a trace of the fire upon the garment of truth which he has worn."

And then Clifford addressed directly the jury of working-men: "I do not put Mr. Littlefield upon this stand as a man of culture—of nice, delicate, moral sense; but I put him here as an honest man who fills reputably his position in life."

Indeed, he went on, it is in just such walks of life that the presumption that men of learning and cultivation could not possibly commit atrocious crimes is most stubbornly ingrained. But the annals of crime are full of exactly such cases: of the schoolmaster Eugene Aram who murdered for money a century before in England; even of a prelate of the Church like Dr. Dodd; even, dare it be said, of a Coolidge in Maine. For it "is out of the

heart not the head that are the issues of life" and all
the learning in the world would not save a man
from wickedness if he were not deeply embedded
in true religion. "Reputation is one thing; character another."

After this rousing crescendo, Clifford descended to the details yet again of boxes and keys,
knives and spots; and most important, of moneys
owing and not paid. Had Dr. Webster truly been
able to discharge his debt from lecture tickets, why
could the defence not bring every one of the students whose fees made up that sum?

And at the end, he returned to the defence's
distinction between manslaughter and murder. It
mattered not a jot, he said, whether the premeditation was one day or one minute. The only provocation that, according to the law, could be considered
justifying the lesser charge was one of blows not
words.

Yes, a coloratura performance, Bemis judged,
bravo, bravissimo.

Then Clifford ruined it.

"If you undertake the prerogative of mercy, how
can you be sure, Gentlemen, what mercy is?" He
then went on to sound a lot like Mayor Bigelow
who had, in an incontinent and vulgar way, complained bitterly that the increase in murders had
been aggravated by the misconceived disposition
of juries to recommend clemency.

"If ever there was a case which required the jury

to stand up firmly to their duty as citizens it is here and now."

What a guy I have been, said Bemis to himself. How could I not have noticed? This is John Clifford's first campaign and I have been his speech writer!

It was ten to five. In the darkening air outside the room the snow had stopped, but when the place was quiet, great rushing gusts of wind were heard blowing through the streets of Boston and against the court-room windows and walls. Would spring never come?

"JOHN WHITE WEBSTER." Chief Justice Shaw's mighty instrument sounded like the tolling bell of a great Gothic cathedral. Even were a prisoner acquitted he would never forget its awful sound.

"Before committing this cause to the jury, if you have anything to add to the arguments which have been urged on your behalf by your counsel, any-thing which you deem material to your defence, by way of explaining or qualifying the evidence against you, you are at liberty now to address it to the jury."

His voice lowered somewhat, attempting to sound the disinterested advisor: "I feel bound to say, however, that this is a privilege of which you may avail yourself or not, at your discretion."

The place had never been so still. Every eye was

on the dock; every person in the galleries and on the floor hoping to see the accused rise; every lawyer, but most especially the counsel for the defence, desperately hoping he would not.

He did so straightaway, standing quite erect and with a voice seemingly unclouded by trepidation: "I am much obliged to Your Honour for this kind permission to make a statement."

Sohier and Merrick were appalled though not surprised. Before the trial, they had received another memorandum from the Professor fussing not about *whether* but merely *when* such a statement ought to be made. He had drawn up a list of the items which he thought such a statement might clarify, namely:

the consent of Dr. P to the sale of the minerals
the note to Dr. P
the modes of access to my rooms but with no *imputation* of anyone
the grapevine and tan
my excitement on arrest

and much more in this vein.

Merrick looked tight-lipped. He had hoped that his closing address would have been enough for John Webster. But from Webster's demeanour it was apparent that he was determined to be a Professor, to give one more lecture, even if it be his last. Merrick thought gloomily of the students he had quietly inquired from about Web-

ster's classroom manner. They had not been
flattering.

"I will not enter into an explanation—though I
have desired much to do so—of the complicated
network of circumstances, which owing to my peculiar position, the Government has thrown
around me and which for many months has been
crushing me. It would require many hours to do so
minutely and I do not know my strength would be
equal to it. But if time were granted to me I could
show what these people were doing and thinking of
at the time they testified against me. I could explain the facts which have been brought up here
against me which in nine cases out of ten have been
completely distorted and to nine-tenths of which I
could probably give a satisfactory answer."

I wonder, thought Sohier, if we had been able to
call him in his own defence whether we should
have chosen to do so. He seems clear-headed
enough, for the moment. But you never know, with
the man, what might happen next.

Just so. The skyrocket suddenly went off.

"On all the points testimony had been placed in
the hands of my counsel; and my innocence would
have been fully established if they had produced it.
They were highly recommended to me and acting
under their direction I have sealed my lips during
my confinement, trusting myself from the first
moment entirely to them. But in their *superior*
wisdom they have not seen fit to bring forward the

evidence that had been prepared for them by me and which would have exonerated me from a variety of these acts which the Government has brought to bear against me with consummate ingenuity but which I hope will not have an undue influence on the jury."

He went on directly to speak of his letter to Marianne and its references to the bundle Mama was not to open and the prosecutors' claim that it contained the mortgage notes. No, they came from elsewhere, this was all to do with some citric acid he had promised his wife and had forgotten to buy.

Citric acid? Sohier forced himself to pay attention. He felt for Merrick, who had reddened above his stiff white collar as the Professor had taken him to task before the class, had set them both in the corner with the dunce's hat. He struggled hard with himself too, gritting his teeth. Do—not—despise—your—client.

Bemis cringed inwardly as though someone had performed an indecent act in front of him. The fact is, he reflected, Merrick had been exceptionally feeble in cross-examination even though Sohier had done his best. But he was also intensely curious as to whether Webster was about to prove the correctness of the Massachusetts statute by plunging into a reckless, unintentional self-incrimination.

Nothing so sensational occurred. Instead, Webster followed a peculiar, inconsequential course around what seemed arbitrarily selected items of the evidence: how the copper nitrate came to be spilled; how Francis Parkman had certainly spoken of his brother's "aberration" of mind; how he often locked himself in his rooms to prevent students doing damage to equipment and chemicals as they had once done; how the money for Dr. Parkman was laid by in a small trunk which he removed the morning of the twenty-third, "but unfortunately no-one saw me take it out before I came over to Boston." All his movements during the week were explainable. That he was eating a mutton chop at Brighams was provable by his new copy of Humboldt's *Cosmos,* which he left there.

God save us, thought Bemis. The man had just slaughtered an old friend and set about dismembering his body and he goes and buys *Humboldt*! And did the very stars still wheel in the heavens?

"And so I might go on explaining a variety of circumstances which have been distorted against me. Many things might have been mentioned, if I had had any thought they would be required; but I had no thought they would be. I depended on the truth alone to show my innocence."

One thing more. "I have felt more distressed by the production of these various anonymous letters than, I had almost said, by anything else that occurred during the trial. And I call God to witness—and if it should be the last word that I should ever speak—I positively declare I never wrote those letters. Since they were introduced into the Case my counsel has received a letter from this very 'Civis' in which the writer says he wrote the one signed with that name. A notice has already appeared in the newspapers I believe calling upon him to come forth but he has not yet shown himself."

And then, in a high, impassioned voice: "If he is present here in the court-room and has a spark of humanity in his breast I call upon him to come forward and declare himself."

Webster tilted his head to look searchingly through the galleries as the room fell hushed; heads turned this way and that not wanting to miss any sign of an arm or a body rising from its place. But none did. After a few more moments of tragic silence, the defendant sat heavily, back into his place. The quiet gave way to a buzz of astonishment.

A recess was called. It was cold and pitch dark outside; stuffy with labour and emotion within.

Though it was already late, the Chief Justice began his charge to the jury. But as soon as he began, his colleagues moved a little closer to him, Justice Wilde looking especially concerned. They were all accustomed to Lemuel Shaw—immense, imperious, impassive—instructing juries or counsels or prisoners in that great baritone instrument unbroken by the least sign of emotion. It was, after all, the Vox Justicia.

But this time, he seemed to have trouble clearing his throat and occasionally he spoke so low that were there another Lemuel Shaw in the room he would undoubtedly have ordered himself to speak up.

"The case has been so long under consideration, it has now been brought to such a crisis, the whole of the evidence and the arguments of counsel standing before you that we feel unwilling notwithstanding the lateness of the hour, to postpone our part of this duty to another day which must necessarily extend the trial into another week; and therefore painful and laborious as this duty is we think that it is best now to proceed to the performance of it in order that you may proceed to the deliberation of your verdict."

He means this night to go on for as long as it must, thought Bemis. The charge, the deliberations, perhaps even a verdict; all to be done with before we see chapel to-morrow morning. He doffed his imaginary hat to the man. Though a Lemuel, a minor prophet, he is after all, a Greek: a man who understands the obligations of tragedy. We must proceed until all is known; a verdict declared; a sacrifice made ready; an atonement decreed.

As he moved up to the altitudes of the law, the Chief Justice's command of his own passions seemed restored. He became authoritative, powerful in voice and argument; at times, immense and majestic, conscious that not only all of Boston, all of the American Republic, but a great part of the world, was attending to all he said. Then, every so often, his tone swooped down from the mountain tops of posterity to the jury box and would adopt a softer, avuncular familiarity. "I am here," it seemed to say, "not to admonish or intimidate you but as your counsellor, your colleague, your friend."

Pungent generalisations flowed from him, as from a great shaman or rabbi called on to edify the perplexed. You wish to know the distinction between murder and manslaughter? Very well, the latter is "homicide mitigated out of tenderness to the frailty of human nature." But such involuntary or malice-free act is incompatible with any evidence of violence done by weapons and is certainly not warranted by provocations of words alone.

At the heart of his charge was the definition of circumstantial evidence because, as he noted, if the case was to be proved at all it would have to be by such connected and correlated evidence. That it should be so ought not unduly concern the jury, for an inconceivable number of violent crimes would go unpunished were they to depend exclusively on the positive evidence of direct eyewitness. And since the nature of such crime was to be committed in secrecy and darkness and its traces covered in disguise, such evidence assumed an even greater importance. If there was no such positive witness, then "a body of facts . . . may be proved of so conclusive a character as to warrant a firm belief of the fact quite as strong and certain as that on which discreet men are accustomed to act in their most important concerns."

Discreet men and important concerns: the appeal was not, in the end, to some impersonal or organically mysterious legal process, something quite external to human belief and habit. No, this was law that seemed, in his formulation, to spring from within our common intuitions. Lemuel Shaw strayed even further from the dry parchment of precedent (though he offered many). His chosen genre when he spoke of circumstantial evidence was poetry. He spoke then, of footprints in the snow that would lead us to the identity of certain beasts or birds; he spoke of a mother delivering in secret a bastard infant later found dead and the presumption that it was born alive. A little later, to show how separate things might be plausibly joined, he related an English case where a cartridge wad was found near a fatal wound. Unrolled and read, it was a half stanza of a ballad, the other half of which was discovered in the pocket of a nearby suspect.

Torn ballads, tracks in the snow, a dead baby; the judge as painter: landscapist, genre master, dramatist. But he could not with images alone avoid, in the end, the fine distinctions expected of his charge.

There were rules governing the weight of such evidence. First, each of the circumstances must themselves be proved; second, each of the facts thus proved must be consistent with each other so that if, for example, by alibi, one fact should prove inconsistent, the entire chain would be broken. And finally, all such facts drawn together and congruent, must lead "on the whole to a satisfactory conclusion producing in effect a reasonable and moral certainty that the accused and no-one else committed the offence charged. It is *not* sufficient that they create a probability though a strong one. . . . [The guilt of the accused] must be proved beyond reasonable doubt excluding suicide and death by the act of any other."

Deeper and deeper into the concentric circles of definition Justice Shaw dove. Though in the subsequent fame and endurance of his ruling on circumstantial evidence its philosophical softness has often been overlooked, this is what lay at the very core: a further definition of "reasonable doubt." What was it? Not possible doubt; rather that "which, after the entire comparison and consideration of all the evidence, leaves the minds of jurors in that condition that they cannot say they feel an abiding conviction, to a moral certainty of the truth of the charge."

An "abiding conviction"? How should a man recognise this "abiding"? Where should it reside? In the pit of his stomach? In places other than the seat of logic? If it were there, might then the "reasonable and moral certainty" be declared to be satisfied?

How might they come to such a conclusion in this case? Were there any circumstances that did indeed break the chain of connexions argued by the Government? The six witnesses produced by the defence to imply that Dr. Parkman was still alive and in town after leaving the College were the most obvious instance. And here, as the law of Massachusetts entitled him to do, Shaw began to weigh the evidence. To many commentators from other state bars, he sounded very much as though he were in fact doing the work of the prosecution, for he drew attention to mistaken imaginings and delusions. If George Parkman, "somewhat peculiar in person and manners," had actually been seen on Friday afternoon, why were there not hundreds and thousands of witnesses come forward to say so?

There were other places too where his gloss on the evidence was heavily partial. The *corpus delicti* indispensable for any kind of charge of homicide had not been proved with certainty from the pathological evidence alone *except* for the dentists' testimony. Dr. Keep's word was given weight; Dr. Morton's dissent, while acknowledged, treated very lightly.

Not that the prosecution's case was wholly followed. The entire evidence about Webster's behaviour following arrest was deemed marginal to determining his guilt for "such are the various temperaments of men and so rare the occurrence of the sudden arrest, . . . who can say how an innocent or a guilty man ought to act?" Nor was the fact that he had waived an examination in a police court following arrest especially significant since the law entitled him to do so without any imputation of guilt. The letters? He thought the proof slight.

Two and a half hours perhaps had passed. The Chief Justice was not yet done. His voice still remained steady and deep. He had already been painter, poet, philosopher. At last, and to the final consternation of the defence, he became detective. In the matter of motive, the matter of money, the jury might want to consider of especial significance one peculiar fact.

What was this? Bemis wondered. Something they hadn't seen; hadn't emphasised?

The mortgage notes found at Dr. Webster's home—not the smaller one, for Dr. Parkman's loan, that which had been inscribed "paid"—but the larger one, for the full two thousand and more dollars owing the rest of the creditors. This was not due for another year. Supposing that the defendant had asked, and the Doctor abruptly surrendered the smaller mortgage note just discharged, why should he have surrendered the *other* along with it?

Earlier in the trial this had been explained as a matter of the Doctor's haste and carelessness. The trouble with such an explanation was that everyone in the room—everyone in Boston—knew full well that if Dr. George Parkman were indeed often hasty he had never in his whole life been known to be careless, least of all about money.

Exceedingly obliged to you sir, thought Bemis, wondering at the same time whether the Attorney General's sentiments at the Justice's supererogation were those of wholly unmixed gratitude.

At last, Lemuel Shaw came to the issue of character. Yes, indeed, it may properly weigh when testimony for and against is so very finely balanced. Should a stranger be accused of a larceny and the community where he is known declare him irreproachable to their certain knowledge, it might well count for him. "But where it is a question of great and atrocious criminality, the commission of the act is so unusual, so out of the ordinary course of things and beyond common experience—it is so manifest that the offence must have been influenced by motives not frequently operating upon the human mind—that evidence of character and of a man's habitual conduct under common circumstances must be considered far inferior to what it is in the instance of accusations of a lower grade. *Against facts strongly proved character cannot prevail.*"

Ah, so the clerk tempted to embezzlement

would be borne up on the strength of family love while the murderer must sink.

It was eight o'clock. Enough had been said. The Chief Justice seemed to agree.

"Gentlemen, when it is said that we may err, it is true. But it is nothing more than to say that we are human. On a subject where absolute certainty cannot be obtained, where moral certainty must always govern, it is always possible to fall into error." (When the trial is over, Bemis wondered, would the Chief Justice take him into his confidence as to how to recognise this "moral certainty" on which he so much depended?)

The jury retired. Looking at Dr. John Webster, sometime Professor of Chemistry, Bemis thought "to fall into error" indeed. I must do so many times each day of my life. But to drop thus, so far, so fast, into darkness and damnation is a Satanic descent.

By habit and by choice Boston takes to its bed early. At the Exchange Coffee House, where more than a hundred out-of-town travellers roomed, they signed an agreement on entry to be in by eleven, the decreed "retiring hour." But on this Saturday night, with the great event yet unresolved, there were precious few guests back in their rooms, and lamps and candles all over the city were burning late. In the chop-houses around Mayor Quincy's market, stubborn customers ig-

nored waiters glaring at them from doorways,
noisily stacking chairs or sweeping sawdust, and
continued to gnaw at their bones or spoon some
warming chowder down their gullets. At the Tremont House, rooms hired for private dinners became blue with cigar fog. Formally dressed men
had lingered all evening over the terrapin soup,
boiled mutton, roast woodcock and blancmange,
and now amidst haw-hawing and solemn grunting,
they lifted snifters to the candlelight to watch the
brandy swirl and wait for news. Closer to the
Court-house, the taverns had filled up with gentlemen of the press sitting out the jury's decision over
tankards of ale and taking bets on how long they
would be kept waiting. Lads had been hired at fifty
cents an hour to stay at the Court-house and sprint
over just as soon as there were signs of a verdict.

Not long after ten, one of these fellows in a cloth
cap came bolting into the Lamb tavern shouting
that the court was to reassemble at a quarter to
eleven. The footsoldiers of the newspapers quickly
mobilised themselves; not one grumbled at having
to leave their mulled wine or porter.

By ten-thirty the court-room was full again;
overflowing in fact, the galleries jammed. The police had given up trying to shut the court-room
doors, so another throng crowded at the rear all the
way down the steps and into the street.

Writing their memoirs (as many did), retired
judges liked to refer to court-houses as "temples of

justice." But the Boston Federal Court was more like the synagogue before the money changers had been cleared: a commotion of busy conversation and freely vented opinions. Over the eleven days of the trial, particular men and women who had sat in reserved places had become accustomed to each other's company, much as on a steamboat passage or a stage-coach journey. They had become familiar with the backs of those in front of them, their bonnet pins or collar studs; neighbouring spectators had obligingly alternated their elbows on the arm-rests of their chairs.

Now they were reassembled, a nervous droning hubbub at a penultimate moment. But as soon as the Clerk of the Court announced a verdict had been agreed, all this noise abruptly stopped. So when John White Webster, with a ghostly pallor on his face, was led to his seat, he was faced with a sea of staring silent eyes.

The jury came in and took, it seemed to everyone, an age shuffling to their seats; after them and with equal ponderousness, the bench.

From the Clerk: "Gentlemen of the Jury, have you reached a verdict?"

Three or four voices replied in a low tone, as if in a church response: "We have."

"Who shall speak for you?"

"The Foreman."

"John W. Webster, hold up your right hand! Foreman look upon the prisoner! What say you Mr.

Foreman, is John W. Webster the prisoner at the bar, guilty or not guilty?"

Byram, the locksmith, hesitated just a moment, as though there might yet be an alternative; Bemis could see his diaphragm rise with a suppressed sigh: "Guilty."

"Gentlemen of the Jury, hearken to your verdict as the Court have recorded it. You upon your oaths do say that John W. Webster the prisoner at the bar is guilty: so you say Mr. Foreman so, Gentlemen, say you all."

The word, then, was sounded twice. At its first enunciation, John W. Webster visibly started; his right hand gripped the rail and his head fell. At the second, his carriage suddenly gave and his body dropped into the chair.

Nothing moved, no sound was heard. A void had opened and swallowed the room with its hundreds of people and hundreds of thousands of words. Minutes passed this way in terrible immobility. While all eyes were concentrated on the man, his own were covered to avoid meeting them. Even when Merrick went to the bar, murmured something of resources not yet tried—a writ of error—John Webster stayed with his head lowered as if his neck would not bear the weight of it.

At last the Chief Justice managed to break from this paralysis and to give a mute order, with a hand, for the court to be cleared; the Clerk barked it out. Men and women began to move off, looking behind them at Webster, still sitting, a handkerchief now over his eyes. Then, in the middle of this foot-dragging, boot-creaking against the plank floor came a sound that was half-cry, half-command, like something wounded and ashamed and angry: "Take me away from this place so that I may not be looked on any longer."

And so they did; and as if released from some spell, the stuffy room became once more a place of human assembly and disassembly from which each in his own way, at last went home.

"What a relief it was to us," wrote one of the jury the next week, "when we were again allowed to 'go free' and rejoin our families and friends after so long and painful a separation! And there was not a Juror's heart but would have leapt for joy could the prisoner have been justly allowed the same unspeakable blessing."

# 7
# Payment Pending:
# The Press, the Preachers
# and the Prisoner

Great fun, the macabre, as confirmed by brisk sales of Ambrose Bierce and Edgar Allan Poe.

A year before he killed George Parkman, John Webster had organised a little after-supper entertainment at his house. At a signal, the maid lowered the gas lamps. Candles were doused, and a bowl of blue phosphorus was brought in, little curls of flame shooting about the glass and throwing unearthly reflections against the walls. Suddenly a shriek came from one of the ladies, for leaning over the bowl, his face livid blue, was her host, a rope about his neck, tongue lolling from a corner of the mouth. A huge joke!

April Fools' Day, 1850. At ten past nine Constable Jones and Jailer Andrews brought the prisoner into the Court-house, his wrists in irons, his expression distraught and sick. Every so often, and at irregular moments, his eyes would shut tight; and

View of the Interior of Professor Webster's Cell

when they opened they rolled wildly about the room or at the ceiling. Dr. Lewis dimly recalled Dr. Parkman having written of such abject melancholic states he had witnessed in Paris.

Confronted with this spectacle of misery, it was hard to keep one's composure; indeed, for many of the principals in the room it was quite impossible. One who was not there, the acid New York lawyer Abraham Oakey Hall, read the reports of the shedding of tears and thought them all "a blubbering set": Dr. Keep crying over his dentures; Littlefield weeping when he found the remains; the jury apparently in tears for over forty minutes before the Foreman could get a vote out of them. (They had spent another two hours in silent prayer.) And this morning the Attorney General, who went through the form of asking for the "sentence which the law of this Commonwealth affixes for this offence" and the Chief Justice, who passed it, both did so with tremulous, lachrymose voices and much dabbing at eyes and cheeks.

Crocodile tears? Listening to Lemuel Shaw, it was difficult to believe so. He began by speaking of "meeting you [the prisoner] here for the last time" as though they were at a class reunion, and then of the indescribable pain he felt at passing the sentence of death. And after going through the conventional summary of the crime and the trial, he lapsed into the voice of the preaching pastor; a mere servant of the Chief of all Justices. On his behalf and that of the sixth commandment, he urged Webster, should he think his punishment too severe,

if one repining thought arises in your mind or one murmuring word seeks utterance from your lips— think, oh think of him instantly deprived of life by your guilty hand; then if not lost to all sense of retributive justice, if you have any compunctious visitings of conscience you may perhaps be ready to exclaim, in the bitter anguish of truth—"I have sinned against Heaven and my own soul; my punishment is just; God be merciful to me a sinner."

There followed more pieties on the terrible example this case might be, especially to the young, to "guard against the indulgence of every unhallowed and vindictive passion." Yet the Chief Justice refrained from issuing the usual words of advice that he freely offered when addressing the more normal species of cutthroat, as he put it, "the illiterate, the degraded, the outcast, whose early life has been cast among the vicious, . . . who have been blessed with no means of moral and religious culture, who have never received the benefits of cultivated society nor enjoyed the sweet and ennobling influences of home." In such a case as this, "where all the circumstances have been reversed," he need not act the moral tutor. The Professor could take his own lessons to heart.

What he was to declare was the voice of the

law and not his own (and indeed anyone who heard Shaw would confirm that it indeed did not sound like him at all). Yet God forbid he should make this merely an official act and not express his sympathy and compassion: "And though we have no word of present consolation or earthly hope to offer you in this hour of your affliction, we devoutly commend you to the mercy of our Heavenly Father with whom is abundance of mercy and from whom we may all hope for pardon and peace!"

With what seemed a great effort, the words of the sentence were uttered: "Removed from this place . . . close custody . . . thence taken at such time . . . to the place of execution, there be hung by the neck."

Another immense silence broken again by sounds from the prisoner's dock—a soft, sobbing lamentation as his forehead fell abruptly against the bar.

To leave the place, he needed two men to support him with their arms, just as he had four months before on the night of his arrest. Outside the court the crowd surged towards him shouting, and he ducked spontaneously as though they might hurt him with their cries, and then, with a strength drawn from somewhere unknown, sprinted like a schoolboy to the waiting police carriage.

.    .    .

## Payment Pending

Another coach delivered the Attorney General back to New Bedford. The following day he wrote to his friend Winthrop.

The long agony is over and I am once more by my own hearthstone trying to restore the equilibrium which two weeks' straining of my entire being had deranged and disturbed—I have never before and can never be again kept up to such an extreme tension—but in looking back and sternly sanctioning my whole course from the commencement of my connection with the case to its close, I cannot find any cause of self-reproach. God knows I have compassionated the poor wretch, almost soulless as he seems to be, & my heart has bled for his family, almost as if they were my own.

Personally I cannot help feeling this trial to have been a great crisis in my life—a failure in it would have been fatal—a moderate degree of success would have been scarcely less unfortunate—and I devoutly thank the Good Being who has guided and strengthened and sustained me through the eminent success which the assurances that I have received from all quarters leave me not at liberty to doubt my having achieved.

I am distressed more than I can express at the awful crucifixion of my argument by the Reporters. There is not one that is tolerable—but it is a Satisfaction to know, and this is the main purpose of my writing, that Dr. Stone has taken a literal phonographic report which is now being stereotyped by Phillips and Sampson & which will be the only authentic report of the Trial. It will make a book of about two hundred pages and will be out in about a week.

For a few days, at least, George Bemis also rested in the satisfaction of what he concluded was a work well done. "Clifford has done me the honor to keep me in constant proximity," he wrote in his journal, "and I have been impressed with his general generosity of purpose and candor of demeanour. We had one misunderstanding when I thought he interfered rather ceremoniously in one of my cross-examinations, but on his explanation and apology (most ample) I fully compromised the slight. So yesterday I thought (to myself) that some public allusion to my aid in his closing might have been appropriate but I do not mean to charge him with intentional engrossment of public praise. And if he be anxious of praise (as I judge he must be) from his flattering encomiums of Sohier and Merrick (the latter in my judgement quite undeserved) I have the charity to remember that he received a large portion of his pay for his great exertions in that coin."

As for his pay, Bemis was looking forward to receiving his thousand-dollar fee from the Reverend Francis Parkman and (despite his grey fatigue at this point) had undertaken to help prepare the Government's argument should a petition for a writ of error be made by the defence. If Clifford's ship was to rise on a tide of public acclaim, then his own small boat, moored alongside, would be borne up on the swell.

A week later it seemed that the both of them might be sunk.

"Travesty," "outrage," "offence against all principles of justice," "abominable arrogance," "the writing, not the execution of law" were some of the terms that filled the newspapers in days and weeks following the verdict. Inside Boston, opinion was mixed. The *Trumpet* and the *Universalist Magazine* rejoiced that "this has been one of the fairest and most impartial trials that we ever attended" and that "although it might have been supposed that given his station and connexions he would have been favoured, to the credit of all concerned, nothing of the sort had taken place."

It was just this kind of sanctimonious crowing that commentators beyond the city and the state found so nauseatingly Bostonian. New Yorkers felt this especially. As the *Sunday Morning News* of that city put it, even though there was widespread feeling as to Webster's guilt, the verdict (not to mention the sentence) was an outrage on the evidence presented and the procedure adopted. Abraham Oakey Hall thought the whole trial "unmistakably Bostonian" in its complacent contempt for hard evidence and its preference for melodrama over due process. What was truly at stake here, he thought, was the self-esteem of an entire

community and the urgency with which they
wanted a disgusting embarrassment put out of the
way:

From the polished brutality of the police officers who
gave evidence that they had studied the tactics of
Newgate to considerable purpose; from the avidity
with which the purse-holders of the deceased entered
into the charge; from the cold-blooded shoulder-
shrugs with which the majority of his fellow-
professors received intelligence of Dr. Webster's
arrest, it would fairly seem that the stake of half a
million of property and the vacancy of a college chair
were the most powerful incentives in this hunt of
expiation and defamation.

No charge of murder could possibly have been
brought, Hall insisted, unless there was *certainty*
(not merely as the Chief Justice proposed) more
than a reasonable doubt, of the *corpus delicti.* But
since the anatomical evidence was so ambiguous,
and even those who presented it conceded they
could not have recognised Dr. Parkman had they
not known he was looked for, the identification all
turned on the evidence of the dentist Dr. Keep.
That this was flatly contradicted by Dr. Morton
(and by dentists from all over the country writing
to the Governor), precluded exactly that certainty
required by the law to uphold the indictment.

Shaw's failure to point this out, as well as his
cavalier dismissal of evidence of witnesses whose

credibility had not been successfully impeached by the prosecution, and his transformation of the conventions regarding circumstantial evidence earned him a place in judicial history alongside Judge Jeffreys and the Bloody Assizes.

There was something not truly American about such a power being allowed to a judge, the *St. Louis Intelligencer* thought. The freedom with which he was allowed to comment unfavourably on evidence, to argue doubtful points with the jury and even to introduce new points (such as the amazing suggestion that chloroform had been used) in effect had made the judge a third prosecuting attorney. The reporter knew, to be sure, that Massachusetts had adopted these practises from the British bar, but had not Americans fought a war precisely to be free from such slavish and partial habits? At least the West would be free. "The laws of Missouri we think are in this respect a great improvement. . . . The judge is prohibited by express statute of this State from giving any instruction or charge to the jury except in writing."

As John Webster became transfigured into victim, who at most might have been convicted of manslaughter, so Littlefield the janitor became villain. The Syracuse *Archimedean* summed up a general sentiment:

We do not pretend to say Dr. Webster is not guilty. But we do pretend to say that no man, however

humble—no criminal however base—no mortal however contemptible (even if sunk to the grade of that
most disgusting of all bipeds, *Ephraim Littlefield*)
ought to be sent to an infamous death on such
testimony.

Look at his behaviour on the witness stand!

Did he approach it with the reverence, the gravity,
the tenderness of one who feels that his words are
about to sweep a fellow-being into eternity—to fall
like a flood of burning lava upon a happy home and
bury under its molten tide a household shrine once
radiant with domestic love, bright with the buds of
Hope and fragrant with the full blown flowers of
Memory? . . . No-one can have read his testimony
without being struck with the flippancy, the self-
conceit, the impertinence, the heartlessness, the un-
ruffled complacency with which his blackguard spirit
runs riot over the ruin of a gentleman. His credibility,
we admit, is not affected by these considerations. We
desire not to pronounce him a perjurer and himself
the murderer of Parkman for we would do no injustice
even to a dog, but we must say that we would not hang
even a dog upon the testimony of Ephraim Littlefield.

Littlefield; the Chief Justice and the rest of the
bench; the aggressive, sarcastic and casuistical
Attorney General; the smug Marshal and his
toy policemen; the professors and doctors with
their disingenuous hand-wringing; the dentists,

chemists, twine-makers and their preposterous self-advertising: they were all as big a pack of hypocrites and scoundrels as had ever flattered themselves with historical self-importance.

Just as dismaying to these critics was the toothless performance of the defence, transparently embarrassed by their client and bound by some incomprehensible act of self-restraint from going after the prosecution's witnesses with the aggression and resoluteness their loosely connected suppositions and inferences deserved. The tigers of the New York bar were lost in chagrin at having been denied the opportunity to show their claws on behalf of judicial fairness.

Nor did the petition for a writ of error do anything to still these angry criticisms, for it was based entirely on procedural technicalities: whether the Sheriff had correctly applied the seal to the indictment, whether the Supreme Judicial Court had automatic jurisdiction over the case and so on. What it did not argue was that the Chief Justice had so misdirected the jury as to invalidate the verdict. It did not do this because, by another sublime irony that caught the attention of out-of-state critics, the body that heard this appeal was identical to the bench that conducted the trial! Was Lemuel Shaw about to criticise Lemuel Shaw for abusing the conventions of the judge's charge; or for that matter, worry unduly about seals applied or misapplied? Grave, decent, incompetent Pliny Merrick, in his moments of wildest optimism, could hardly have supposed so.

Shaken by the ferocity of the criticisms, all the principals of the trial (except the convicted murderer) collaborated in an enterprise to produce an agreed version of the proceedings. The Chief Justice was particularly concerned to erase embarrassing references to chloroform; to convert his lapidary remarks on "moral certainty" and "abiding convictions" into something more powerful regarding circumstantial evidence. The Attorney General and Messrs. Sohier and Merrick were all to offer their drafts, and George Bemis was the workhorse appointed to write the reconciled version. Going at it twelve hours a day, six days a week; his coughing fits becoming more violent as the spring released pollen into the humid air; there were times he thought it a Sisyphean labour. No sooner would he offer what he imagined a final version to the counsels or to the bench (especially the bench) than they would find yet another detail to quibble over, or indeed scrawl their rewriting over his proof. He shouldered this thankless burden nonetheless, because he knew that posterity, fascinated with the crime, would demand some sort of definitive history armoured with irrefutable documentation and authoritative appendices. He could already imagine the volume: *Bemis's Report of the Case of John W. Webster,* some six hundred pages thick, bound in crimson cloth or morocco, reposing on the shelves of generations of lawyers, taking its place among the great case histories of American justice.

Such an authoritative record was needed to still the agitation over John Webster's fate. Far from dying away as the trial receded, it had become more intense. The warmer weather had brought the cholera plague back with dreadful force. As the dead departed in plain burial wagons for the cemeteries at the Neck, more of the living arrived from Ireland, swelling the tenements and creating conditions where the bacillus would be welcome to stay awhile longer. Boston was in trouble. Mayor Bigelow was much given to jeremiads about the decay of morals and collapsing of good order occasioned by the new unwashed in his city. And the preachers were in full throat, seeing in the Webster case a sure sign that Boston was the new Babylon, sunk in avarice, rage, whoring and drink.

The Reverend Lyman Whiting preached a sermon entitled "Sin Found Out" on this topic in the Congregational Church at Lawrence: Harvard, "our ancient and Honoured University, mourns in afflictive disgrace." Dr. Webster had gone from "the delightful and decorated dwelling to the cheerless stone cell. Alas! What a change one sin has made. How terrible its finding out. My hearers, the hand of God is in this. The Almighty finger is writing a lesson in this dark drama. That lesson you and I, the community, the nation, the world ought to learn. It is a stain upon human nature not easily washed out."

Others asked where did the guilt truly affix itself? To the dead man, so consumed by vindictiveness and intransigence that he pushed a person of morbid nervousness over the brink? To the men of the law who had so botched the trial? To the whole city where money was so idolised that it would generate such evils?

The writ of error was duly heard by those it criticised and was lightly brushed aside. But each time that some sort of finality was proclaimed, new uncertainties reappeared. All that would spare John Webster execution would be a pardon granted by the Governor and his council. What were the grounds to be?

No legal proceedings could shake the faith of the Webster family in the unblemished innocence of the Professor. When the Prescotts had brought the news of the verdict out to Garden Street on the morning following the trial, Mrs. Webster had been so paralysed with horror that she could say nothing; Marianne had thrown herself into a wild keening, and the other girls had crumpled in sobbing misery. But a resumed indignation at the injustice that had been done together with a resolution to help their afflicted father did something to revive them. Together with a diminishing circle of faithful friends—Charles Cunningham, the Prescotts, Fanny Longfellow—they brought the Doctor comforts: baked goods from home; some lavender water. Ned Sohier brought cigars. Dr. Webster busied himself with an intensive reading program and with preparing his own petition of pardon, based on the notes he had given Sohier and Merrick and which they had declined to present as evidence.

There were signs, too, that should all else fail, he was attending to his spiritual welfare. For towards the end of May he began regular conversations with a minister of the Unitarian Church in Roxbury, George Putnam. On the twenty-third of that month, George Parkman's remains were taken from the vault beneath Trinity Church and transferred to Mount Auburn Cemetery, and in the afternoon Putnam spoke with a new firmness to his charge. There was, he said, "one barrier to our free communication": the knowledge he must have had about Dr. Parkman's fate and which, still undisclosed, must be "an oppressive and intolerable burden." The time had now come for it to be shared.

Perhaps, at last, John Webster could tell the truth. Perhaps. For the only version of the confession elicited by George Putnam is the one the minister himself brought to the Governor's Council on Pardons on July 2. In the meantime, John

Webster's own petition for clemency, based on his continuing insistence of innocence, had been withdrawn.

Yet even as related by Putnam, the statement has, in essence, the ring of truth. It narrated the harassment for debt; the appointment with Dr. Parkman made so that Dr. Webster could implore him for more time, for the sake of the family. When Dr. Parkman arrived on that Friday afternoon,

He called me a liar and a scoundrel and heaped upon me the most opprobrious epithets and taunts. As he shouted at me he drew the two notes for the money I owed him and an old letter from Dr. Hosack, a letter in which Dr. Hosack congratulated Dr. Parkman on getting me appointed as a professor of chemistry.

"I got you into your position and now I will get you out of it!"

I cannot tell how long the torrent of threats and invectives continued. I cannot begin to recall all that Dr. Parkman said to me in those moments. At first I kept trying to interject comments in the hope of pacifying him, but I could not stop him and soon my own anger was aroused. At that point I felt nothing but the sting of his words. I grew furious.

While he was speaking and gesturing in the most violent and menacing manner—thrusting Dr. Hosack's letter in my face—I seized whatever thing was nearest me, a stick of wood, and dealt him a blow with all the force passion could summon. I did not know, nor think nor care where I should hit him nor how hard nor what the effect should be.

He fell to the floor instantly. He did not move.

I knelt beside him. Blood flowed from his mouth and I got a sponge and wiped it away. I got some ammonia and held it to his nose. I spent ten minutes in attempts to resuscitate him but he was dead.

In my horror I ran to the doors and bolted them. A terrible awful panic engulfed me. What should I do?

It never occurred to me to go for help, to tell what had happened. All I could see was the need to conceal Dr. Parkman's body in order to avoid the blackest disgrace.

Then followed a recounting of his dragging the body to the back room, stripping clothes, burning them; removing all Parkman's possessions, later throwing a watch over the Craigie Bridge; dismembering the corpse with the bowie knife; distributing the parts in different places and cleaning the area to efface the slightest trace of blood.

What had the weapon been? A stump of grapevine that he had brought to the College for an experiment showing how wood could take on the color of certain chemicals.

The whole deed, terrible as it was, had been entirely unpremeditated. He had picked up the *two* notes without thinking and even more bizarrely pocketed them rather than burned them. If there had been premeditation why should he have called expressly at Parkman's house that morning to make the appointment; why make it for his own premises?

Had he written any of the letters? Only the crudest note, from East Cambridge.

At the end of it all, so Dr. Putnam reported, he had solemnly asked John Webster to answer "as a dying man, truthfully," did he never have a thought that the death of Dr. Parkman would be an advantage to him?

"No, never," Webster cried. "As I live and as God is my witness I was no more capable of such a thought than one of my innocent children. I never had the remotest idea of injuring Dr. Parkman until the moment the blow was struck. Dr. Parkman was extremely severe and sharp-tongued, the most provoking of men and I am irritable and passionate. A quickness and violence of temper has been the besetting sin of my life. I was an only child, much indulged, and I have never acquired the control over my passions that I should have acquired early and the consequence of it all is this."

Is this it, then, the truth of the case, that ultimate nugget of certainty that historians once imagined they would find if only they looked hard and long enough in the archives? Can a man truly be slain with a stump of grapevine? And what actually was it, this lethal piece of timber? Though the confession initially had it as an item for experimental demonstration, Webster had added a "supplemental note" in which he changed his mind and said all the grapevines had been brought to the

College to be burned for ash that would fertilise his garden. Ashes to ashes.

Can a man be killed *instantaneously* with a blow from a piece of wood? Impossible, said one set of doctors who came to testify to the Council; quite possible, if not likely, said another set, citing the fragility of the temples and Dr. Parkman's particularly brittle cranial structure.

But just think of this man, said members of the Council. Think of what we know by his own admission: such a creature as this managed to play whist, go to evening parties, read Milton, give lectures, carve the Thanksgiving turkey, even as he was mutilating and burning, forging a letter, and concocting an abominable deception. Would such a monster as this not hesitate to lie once more if he thought it would rescue him from the gallows?

No, think rather of his family, said just one other member of the Council, Benjamin Goode. For three days after the first hearing, Mrs. Webster had appeared dressed in mourning black before the committee, along with all three daughters. Her face, below the black lace, was wet with tears; the girls struggled bravely to bear the immense weight of their anguish.

On July 19, Lieutenant-Governor Reed gave Governor Briggs notice that with only one dissenting vote the committee had voted to reject the petition for clemency.

# 8

# Settlements:
# The Legatees

*Not that he is of high degree*
*We ask you him to save*
*Not that he is a useful man*
*Pardon for him we crave*
*Not that his virtuous loving wife*
*Still unto him doth cling*
*And feels that she would part*
    *with life*
*From death to rescue him*
*Not that three lovely daughters*
    *plead*
*With many a bitter tear*
*And humbly look to God and you*
*To save their father dear*
*But save him O for justice's sake*
*And for our country's fame*
*The honor of the Commonwealth*
*And for your own good name*

My own good name! What do I care for that, thought the Governor. Just give me my horse and my chickens and keep reputation. But the poem is really quite commendable in its sentiments. And it scans, more or less: dee-da-dee-da-dee-da-dee-da. He opened a box labelled "Petitions," unwrapped the pink ribbon and set the verse on top of others whose contents and authors he knew by heart, for there wasn't a day when he didn't peruse them, however crazy or illiterate.

Some, like Mr. Pearce of Fayetteville in North Carolina, pleaded insanity, for he couldn't imagine how someone could both premeditate a murder (as convicted) and call at the victim's house to solicit an interview on a day of public lectures and not be manifestly demented. The Governor wasn't sure of Mr. Pearce's own grip though, because he had added that the real problem with Webster was that he was excessively absorbed in *Cosmos* and "perchance overvalued the things of this world."

Then there were those, in their different fashions, who were militantly opposed to capital punishment. Charles Spear, the leader of the campaign, had asked him for a stay until further petitions could be brought. And he had granted it, and to be sure petitions had come from New Hampshire, Connecticut, New York, but not in such overwhelming numbers—still less with overpowering reasons—to set aside the execution. To all the philosophico-ethical passions mustered in those arguments he still preferred the simple soul

who had asked him "to take care of his Disconso-
late Wife and Daughters and know that hanging
him won't fetch the dead to life."

With that he had, alas, no quarrel. He wasn't
even sure, if the matter were ever to come to a
vote, how he would decide, for his Baptist God
was, variously, a stern Jehovah and a forgiving
Redeemer. But he was, or had been, like almost all
those in politics, a man of the law; and the statute
was the statute. Nothing in the record of the trial,
not the fiercest provocation offered by George
Parkman, he thought, could make this anything
other than a murder for which the penalty was
unequivocally prescribed.

Well, the task, however loathsome, was his; he
could not evade it.

Perhaps, next year, I shall be set free, he
thought. And something inside George Briggs
made a little jump, like the trout clearing the
surface of the Housatonic.

He reached for his pen.

*August 29, 1850*

A conspiracy of silence had been organised
among George Putnam, Sheriff Eveleth and John
Webster to keep the execution date from Harriet
and the girls. Putnam, who was not a sentimental

man (quite the opposite in fact), was impressed by
this last act of unselfishness on the condemned
man's part. The minister liked to think of himself as
the instrument of a true atonement; a pastor who
had shown a pathetic sinner the way to redemption; who could say, perhaps even to Paradise.

Webster had already made some amends; writing to Pliny Merrick to ask forgiveness for having
so churlishly repudiated his counsel in court. With
Ned Sohier, who visited many times a week and
who showed the sincerest concern for his family,
he knew he need not make any formal apology.
Sohier understood the desperation that had caused
Webster to offend in such a way; but better, he
seemed to understand the horrible flux that had
made him into a raving brute. It had been, he now
knew, a chemical alteration. The word that came to
his mind over and again was *ebullition*. How many
times had he used it in his lectures when discussing
the boiling point of liquids or the reaction of acids
and alkali? That had been the rage in his blood; a
foaming, bubbling turmoil that forced its way over
the rim of his vessel and scalded whatever was in
its way.

Images of glass bottles with vehemently froth-
ing fluids came into his mind, himself standing
before the students explaining as best he could in
the midst of their boyish noisiness; more images,
this time line engravings in the pages of his child's
history book, of Vesuvius in eruption pouring lava

down onto sinful Herculaneum below. Was that why in the forged letter written in his childish hand he had spoken of the vessel "herculan" to which the Doctor was supposed to have been abducted? More images still, of himself with a stick raised against a college friend, frantic with hatred that he had lost a game of tipping the hat; worse, later, waving a razor against a man who had joked at a barbershop that he had never seen a monkey shaved!

Why had no one told him before; someone versed in these matters of mental disorder, that that was what he suffered from: periodic attacks of ebullition? Oh he knew it was an old-fashioned term, gone out of favour, but who knew better than he its scientific precision? The Erving Professor of Chemistry had had the property of being changed, chemically, from good to evil. Now the process would be reversed, this time metaphysically.

There had been so much time. Now there seemed so little. He wondered how his letter of sorrow and contrition, addressed to Francis Parkman, had been received. He had tried, even at the trial, to hold out his hand to the Reverend but knew it would not be taken. He knew too, that of all that family, it was the churchman who perhaps was most adamant that he be punished to the letter of Hebraic law. Well, he could understand that too; he hoped only to make Francis Parkman understand the truth, that until his brother began the persecution, he had felt nothing but gratitude to him. Would he ever comprehend that?

If there were one thing more he would have wished for it was a little solitude. But orders had been given, usual for these occasions he understood, never to leave the condemned man by himself. Even at this minute, Mr. Andrews was sitting on his stool at the other end of the cell reading the *Transcript.* What would be said about him on the morrow, he wondered? Nothing so cruel it would lacerate his poor bereft girls.

Ah, of all the deceitful countenances he had contrived these last months, the hardest was this very evening. They had brought him dried flowers from Fayal, whose scent had called him back to that blessed island, some of his favourite nougat de Montelimar and a volume of Longfellow's verses. The necessary charade almost broke down when Mr. Andrews told him there was a crowd gathering on Leverett Street and he thought the news had become public after all. But the good-hearted jailor had made up some story about a load of fuel being delivered and invited them to leave through his quarters instead.

At another moment, too, he thought they must somehow have known, though there was nothing on their faces to show it. For by some small miracle they had reached, in their daily readings of the Gospel, I Corinthians 15, and when Marianne reached the passage that began "O death, where is thy sting? O grave, where is thy victory?" he had rested his chin on the dark head of his little Catherine, and a great stream of tears had fallen on her crown.

*August 30, 1850*

A delectable summer night in Boston; velvety warmth and the stars like studs glinting in the blackness.

All the afternoon, as it became known that John Webster had been hanged at the jail, crowds—immense and sometimes unruly—had gathered in front of the gates at Mount Auburn Cemetery. It had been the condemned man's wish to be interred there, and the newspapers had duly reported this. Cambridge had never seen such traffic. After carriages had dropped some folks off by the cemetery gates, they took others for a drive about the Common to catch a glimpse of the murderer's house, to marvel at the apparent ordinariness. How could black-eyed Susans grow in such profusion about a place stained by sin and crime?

But no hearse, nor nothing like it, nor even a suspiciously laden cart ever appeared. Even so, some who insisted that it would arrive under cover of darkness settled down to spend the night if need be, in anticipation of the thrilling moment.

No one was looking for a waggon with a coffin hidden aboard going in quite the other direction, away from Leverett Street, down towards the docks and north to Copp's Hill. Ned Sohier's son, a pleasant boy called Will, drove the horse, neither too slowly nor too quickly, the hooves clattering on the cobbles. Close to the cemetery path, halfway up the hill there was a space amidst the stones. Andrews the jailor set a dim lamp by it and the three men dug as fast as they could, lumps of turf flying against the moonlit sky. When they had done Ned Sohier paused for a moment on his shovel, his whole body hot and wet with the work. Were his fellow beings so truly abandoned that the three men had to go through this elaborate subterfuge to avoid the desecration of a grave? He remembered what John Webster had told him about Ephraim Littlefield. That he had never doubted. The possibilities sent a shiver through his frame.

Together the men lifted the heavy box towards the hole. For a second Andrews lost his footing, sending the coffin swinging sharply to Ned Sohier. To keep his balance and prevent it from falling, he found himself embracing the upright box, his cheeks pressed against the roughly planed wood for a full minute before the others helped him, very gently, to lower it into the dirt.

· · ·

Amelia Hickling Nye to her sister, Mary Anne Ivens

New Bedford, 4th October 1850

Dear sister,

I went to see Harriet and the girls on September 3rd and found them all very calm and resigned and before I left they were almost cheerful. They spoke a great deal about the Dr.'s penitence and sincere repentance. They think there never was such a being, they say his nature was heavenly and his face actually shone and was radiant. It is true that he suffered punishment in the eyes of the world but they think he was saved and do not look on his cell as anything gloomy but as a temple where they spent so many hours administering comfort to their father. I have copied a prayer and a dream he composed for them to say after his funeral. I wanted to copy his last letter to his family but Marianne said that was sacred and indeed she did not like my having copied the dream and the prayer. He made no further confession but one half of the people in Boston believe it was a premeditated act and for that reason his sentence was not commuted. It is far better for the family that the Law should have had its course. They will be better off without him. The people in Cambridge have been extremely kind and considerate to the family and all express the hope they will not leave Cambridge.

Harriet is so naïve about the world's opinion as she never looks into a newspaper. It was solely on her account that the confession was made public for neither she nor the children would believe him guilty and refused to see anyone who thought him so. Harriet ordered Sister Prescott and anyone else to forbid their houses to anyone who thought him guilty. Poor Sister Prescott has been a martyr for she has been harassed all the time by hearing the Dr.'s praises sung in her ears continually when she knew all the time he was a guilty man. Had it not been for William's delightful letters I think she could not have stood it. She looked almost sick but since the execution she is relieved of a load and before I left Boston I could see how much better she looked.

I must tell you now the family were kept in ignorance of the execution. They went in to see the Dr. the day before as usual and he commanded himself so well that he did not betray himself that that was the last time he should see them on earth.

Mr. Sohier went in to see the Dr. after the family left, he says he never saw such agony as the poor man was in. Dr. Putnam was with him until nine and early the next morning he was with him some time alone. Then the officers and persons invited to be witnesses all came near the cell, Dr. Webster kneeling in the middle of the cell, Dr. Putnam standing in the doorsill offered a prayer in which at Dr. W's request he prayed that people's hearts might be softened towards him and for the bereaved family of the Parkmans. Dr. Putnam, as soon as all was over went to Cambridge to notify the family. Dr. W gave directions for his coffin and who he wished to lay him out. It was his wish to be conveyed to his home that evening and the funeral take place on Sunday but everyone told him it would never do so he gave it up and so did the family. The jailor, thinking that the family would come to the cell to see him, placed the coffin in an angle of forty-five degrees so that the blood went down and he was not discolored in the least and even had a smile on his countenance. Harriet signed a paper giving up the body to Mr. Sohier for interment. All day Saturday and Sunday there were crowds of people in Cambridge waiting for the funeral. A carriage with a lady and two children actually stopped at the door [of the house] to gain admittance to see the wretched man but Nancy fortunately was there and told them there was nothing to be seen and asked them if they were not ashamed to come and disturb so afflicted a family. The lady was from New York.

Amelia Hickling Nye to Mary Anne Ivens

February 9th, 1851

His death has been a great relief to them. Harriet has not been as happy now for years—the manner of his death alone clouds her brow occasionally. . . . It will be a long time before they can learn economy. They live nearly as well now as they have ever done and when they have a little money know not how to save it. Since Sam's arrival [Samuel Dabney, engaged to Harriet] they are a great deal in Boston, much to the surprise of everyone who meets them, and Kate says that in a few years they will have the property their grandfather left them and it will not be requisite for them to work, but I think it more to their credit to do something for their living.

Harriet too is out to her new house and grounds. I thought the disgraceful death of her husband would have deterred her from being seen abroad.

Mr. Appleton tried to raise $20,000 for them, they to have the interest and principal to go to the donors at their death—but could find no-one to second his views so he and others made them a present of $5,000—Mr. K bought them a house for $2,500!

Harriet is allowed $450 out of the wreck of her husband's property and the girls were allowed to retain everything that has been given them and when Hatty marries Sam, property left the girls by their grandpa will be sold for benefit and money put out at interest on which they must try to live. They will have altogether over $10,000! I hope you do not think me unkind for speaking in this way but you know I have been poor and can see where they are extravagant. After they leave the house there will be an auction of all the useless and superfluous articles which have been accumulating for years and which cost a great deal of money.

Had the Dr. been imprisoned for life it would have been much worse for them. Then they would have never realised their unfortunate situation and he would have contrived some way of being sick that he might see them. It would have been a living death to all of them. But why do I constantly refer to this painful subject? I meant to banish it from my mind. I believe we feel worse than they do, they look on his death as beautiful but as I do not feel so clear about his being truly penitent I cannot help shuddering when I think of him.

Amelia Hickling Nye to Mary Anne Ivens

December 1853

I saw Harriet laid in her tomb in Cambridge. You cannot think how much more pleasant it was to lay her there with her children [the daughters were at the funeral] than if her husband had been there but it was feared someone would desecrate his tomb for the sake of taking an impression of his features to have a wax figure made to be shown about the country. They did send one round but as it did not resemble him no-one visited him and it was given up.

The weather is terrible, eight or ten below zero . . . the poor have suffered the high price of provisions; here in New Bedford the snow drifts badly; it was fifteen or sixteen feet high in places. One day the milkman could not bring his milk to his customers. The richest man in town, John Avery Parker died in December.

The Millerites expect the world to end sometime in May.


The Millerites got it wrong, again. The Century of Progress turned another notch on its wheel. History stopped telling stories and aspired to science. Romanticism was elbowed aside by positivism: the certainty of an ultimately observable, empirically verifiable truth. Sometimes such truths might be secured by indirect and inadvertent paths; by the pursuit of clues: the variety of finches' plumage, the revelation of microbial organisms beneath a lens, a hair picked up on the tread of a boot, a calligraphic idiosyncrasy, the curve of a cuticle on a Sienese madonna's forefinger. Forensic science replaced the inspired hunch, and logical deduction made the fortune of Sir Arthur Conan Doyle. Professional policemen were replaced by watches, the town by the metropolis, communities by classes, tribes by empires, the cavalry colonel by the general staff officer, fast sail by omnipotent steam; and the seamstress by the sewing machine. The great Railroad Jubilee of 1851 was honoured by the presence of both President Fillmore and Lord Elgin. An immense tent exhibiting the greatest marvels of the mechanical arts and industries was set up on the Common and the procession featured not only splendidly uniformed Massachusetts horse and artillery but an artificially erupting volcano, pulled on a waggon and representing the Etna Company, manufacturers of the very latest and most efficient explosive shells.

Already the *New York Globe* was able to boast that its account of the Webster trial, "reported expressly by its intelligent, active and attentive Reporters," had been "sent over the wires of Morse's Telegraphic line. Great praise is due to the Agents of the *Globe* in Boston and to the Operators at both terminations of the line."

*All hail to Morse! the first to lead*
*The electric fluid round the earth*

*Our country boasts the daring deed*
*And glories that gave him birth*

Vigorous attempts were made to pull Harvard into this bracing new age. In 1850 a report of the Massachusetts Legislature, written by a young Democrat, George Boutwell, declared that "the college fails to answer the just expectations of the people of the state." Of what use was an education of classics or history, other than to a self-perpetuating aristocracy? The College should, instead, be making "better farmers, mechanics or merchants." Professorial pay should be tied entirely to the size of their classes. "The result would be that only those would succeed who taught in departments and in a manner acceptable to the public. That which was desired would be purchased and that which was not, would be neglected."

Despite publicly declining to serve, George Briggs was nominated once more as the Whig candidate for governor. Rural Baptist though he was, somehow he had come adrift from his constituency. For in the fall election of 1850, the Whigs, badly split over the Webster-Clay compromise, failed to gain a majority in the polls. The election went to the Legislature, where a coalition of Free-Soilers and Democrats made Boutwell governor. This coalition was described by its wounded enemies as unholy because it brought together Irish Catholics and rural Calvinists, neither of whom much liked Unitarians, or for that matter, Harvard College.

The following May a new act altered the composition of Harvard's Board of Overseers (though far less radically than Boutwell would have liked), giving a majority to thirty members elected from the Massachusetts House and Senate. The College took this in its stride. Courses in animal husbandry and accounting did not yet feature prominently in the curriculum. But outside scholars were sometimes invited to lend new energy to jaded offerings. In 1852 President Sparks asked Francis Parkman, Jr. (his old student), to serve as a member of the Harvard Committee for Examining History, thus giving "encouragement to your favorite subject by your countenance and aid."

The following year Sparks retired and was succeeded in the presidency of Harvard College by Professor James Walker, the Unitarian minister of the Second Church in Charlestown. His declared motto was "We are not ashamed to improve," and his sermons were great public occasions. At his inauguration there was a good spread but no fireworks. Echoing sententious noises coming from Oxford, he insisted in his inaugural address, "The radical difficulty in modern society may be expressed, it seems to me in two words—'intellectual anarchy.'"

Charles W. Eliot, who would be the greatest of all presidents of American universities, thought that year the moment when Harvard hit rock bottom.

During his term President Walker became severely arthritic and stone deaf. He established music in the college curriculum. A little later a fund was specially endowed to prevent improvident professors from ever again seeking desperate remedies.

In 1857 the skeleton of a mastodon was taken from the Medical College Museum and reinstalled in a new Anatomical Museum together with plaster casts of the *Discobolus*, the *Venus de Medici* and the *Venus de Milo*. Dr. Jeffries Wyman, who had testified for both the prosecution and the defence at Dr. Webster's trial, now judged the mastodon to have been incorrectly assembled and proceeded to reconstruct it according to the best knowledge of pre-historic anatomy.

## CLASS NOTES

BEMIS, George (A.B. '35). Continued to suffer poor health, with tubercular haemorrhages in 1858. Instructed by his physician to live in a more hospitable climate, he settled on the Côte d'Azur and published *American Neutrality, Its Honorable Past, Its Expedient Future.* Deceased, 1876; his estate endowed the Bemis Chair in International Law.

## Settlements: The Legatees

CLIFFORD, John H. (L.L.D. '53). Attorney General, he was elected Whig Governor for the 1853–1854 term. Declining to serve again, he was reappointed Attorney General. Member of the Board of Overseers of Harvard College, 1854–1859. He became, in 1867, President of the Boston and Providence Railroad. Deceased, 1876.

MERRICK, Pliny (A.B. '14). Justice of the Court of Common Pleas, he was appointed to the Supreme Court of the Commonwealth by Governor Clifford. Always associated in the public mind with the Webster case. When he slipped on the ice in front of Barnstable Court, broke three ribs and was waiting, in much pain, for the arrival of the physician, a well-meaning janitor, in an attempt at consolation, said, "Well, Justice Merrick, how thankful you must be it isn't the Chief Justice."

SHAW, Lemuel (A.B. 1800). Produced, in 1852, his own corrected account of the charge to the jury in the Webster case. Cited through the generations as the classic definition of the requirements of circumstantial evidence, it differs in significant respects from both the stenographic record and the authorised report edited by George Bemis '35.

A member of the Board of Overseers, 1831–1853; President of Phi Beta Kappa, 1832–1837; founding trustee of the Museum of Comparative Zoology, 1859; enthusiast of the Massachusetts Historical Society; President of the Society for Propagating the Gospel among the Indians, 1837–1861; Fellow of the American Academy of Arts and Sciences; proprietor of the Boston Athenaeum. A strong believer in the Henry

Clay–Daniel Webster Compromise, he incurred the violent displeasure of the Free-Soilers and abolitionists for upholding the legality in Massachusetts of the Fugitive Slave Act. Under this ruling, in 1854 Anthony Burns was ordered to be returned, and a riot at Faneuil Hall resulted. When Burns was escorted from the state, shops closed, their fronts draped in black, and a coffin was hung suspended over State Street.

Retired from the Supreme Court in 1860, his eightieth year. Enjoyed filling his scrapbook with materials on locust plagues and soap made from potatoes; lectured to the American Academy on the art of splitting granite with wedges. His daughter Elizabeth married Herman Melville in 1850 and the retired Justice much enjoyed terrifying his grandchildren with vivid impressions of a roaring lion. Deceased, 1861, and buried in Mount Auburn Cemetery; his last coherent words are reported to have been "Gentlemen of the Jury."

SOHIER, Edward Dexter (A.B. '29). A memorial meeting of the Suffolk County Bar Association was held in May 1888 to mourn the passing, and mark the life and work of one of its most esteemed members. Several of the deceased's classmates, including Mr. Oliver Wendell Holmes, were present, and resolutions were passed signifying the Bar's high esteem for Mr. Sohier's professional skills and undeviating personal integrity. It was recalled that his dress was unique, his manner cordial and his disposition always frank and especially warm towards younger members of his profession. After fifty years of celebrated successes he recalled only one true failure, the Webster case, and that, he said, because he never could quite rely on his client.

Despising every form of meanness and trickery, he was, in Mr. Holmes's resolution, "above all things a lawyer, neither seeking office nor willing to accept when tendered."

George Parkman, Jr., became involved in an angry exchange with George Putnam over aspersions he considered cast against his father's memory in John Webster's confession. That document he dismissed as a monstrous act of pretended atonement. To imply that his father had ever been given to harshness or that he pursued his debtors, young Parkman insisted, was a wicked calumny. The Reverend George Putnam declined to withdraw the remarks on behalf of Dr. Webster.

Not long afterwards George Parkman, his mother and his invalid sister moved away from No. 8 Walnut Street and bought a house on Beacon Street. George never married and developed something of a reputation for being a recluse, even an eccentric, who insisted on doing his own shopping at the market and on walking briskly all over town.

History's perpetuities, though, can be abridged. The route of the Parkman perambulations is no longer what it was. The West End of Boston has disappeared in its entirety, with the exception of the Harrison Gray Otis House and the Old West Church, which stand like museum pieces amidst some of the ugliest institutional building in America, much of it housing civil servants. Where the house built by Samuel Parkman stood at Bowdoin Square, there now rises an immense brick-faced confection, complete with post-modern Tuscan roof, and gaudy decoration faintly reminiscent of Phineas Barnum's lodging Iranistan. A large flag offering "Space to Let" is draped from its top stories.

The Leverett Street jail was demolished, but the Charles Street jail, built on Parkman land, was still in use until very recently.

Nothing remains of the old Harvard Medical College on North Grove Street. Its successor occupies an immense domain around Longwood Avenue at the border between Boston and Brookline. Where the old College stood, hard by the mudflats of the Charles, there are now stores, office buildings and a large sign inviting customers to sample the celebrated Buzzy's Roast Beef. The intrepid and the curious visitor wandering amidst the labyrinth of the Massachusetts General Hospital (a town in itself) may stumble by mistake on a dark corridor lined with photographs looked at by nobody. One of them has a fuzzy grey picture of a two-story brick building set on piers, with sheds and outbuildings giving onto the river. A brief caption indicates this was the old Medical College, but no one quite recalls just when it was pulled down.

Two houses remain in my mind: the beginning and the end of a history.

One of these houses I imagine set high on a cone-shaped hill overlooking a bay in the Azores. White-washed stucco with a Manueline-Portuguese gable, its walls are surrounded by cloudy blooms of blue hydrangea. The fragrance of tangerine blossom fills the garden. At night wild asses bray, standing in clumps of wild azalea that dot the hillside. Not much happens in such a place. An old lady in a straw hat and white cotton dress buttoned high at the neck in an old-fashioned way sits beneath a parasol passing a needle through her embroidery. Beneath her feet, below the soil, deep below in the blue-black ocean, the rock-bed shifts in imperceptible distances, tilting and pressing, pulling and pushing.

The other house sits in blessed neglect, well off the beaten path of Harvard University tours. Its paint is flaking badly and has discoloured to the point where it is hard to tell if it is a dusty pink or a drab beige. Its details work the memory: twin pairs of pilasters framing the door and set out at the steps, trying hard to give the little house a touch of classical importance; the timbered Gothic dormer window. There were once delphinium in the garden, an arbour of grapevines and a sturdy growth of pink azalea that seemed different from the standard American varieties. But nothing stands in the yard now except cars in need of paint jobs.

At the front door are many names and signs reading: THE FOLLOWING ARE NOT HERE. Owned by the hotel next door, and vigilantly rent-controlled, the place is decomposing. Tenants say the hotel is eager to have it pulled down. One day, of course, it will have its way. The pilasters will surrender to the bulldozer. Windows haunted by the white faces of three girls anxiously scanning a catcalling crowd will be smashed to shivers; the entire fabric of its history pulverized to dust and expelled into the air.

Pittsfield, November 1851

MY DEAR DAUGHTER!

You have probably seen in the papers that the elephant Columbus fell through the bridge in South Adams and was so injured that he died afterwards in Lenox. His owners, thinking the town of Adams might be liable to them for damages, did me the favor to retain me and place the case in my hands with a pretty handsome retainer. What the town will do about it remains to be seen. The animal was valued at fifteen thousand dollars. The owner says he would not have taken that for him and that he cannot be replaced for any sum. He was, I believe, the largest in America. Tell the junior branch of the firm on Bank Corner if he will look up the law and settle the question whether the town is liable for not having a bridge strong enough to hold up an elephant weighing five tons, he may see the elephant for nothing almost.

Your affectionate father,

George N. Briggs

Pittsfield, December 5, 1852

MY DEAR DAUGHTER!

Came back home on Tuesday. All well as usual. Nothing new except my dream last night: I thought I set off for the village and when I entered the road at the east end of our avenue, I found myself standing in the air just above the tops of the trees with my face towards the village. It was night; but a few rays of light shot forth from the east, of inconceivable brightness. They struck the steeple and the cross of the Baptist meeting house and made them perfectly transparent. Retaining their shape they looked as though they were composed of millions of diamonds. A low tower at the right of that had much the same appearance. While I was thus standing with perfect ease and composure in the air, a wagon-load of people in the street below me and a little to the left stopped and looked up at me with seeming surprise. They saw me distinctly as the light from the east shone in my face but they did not turn round to see the wonderful and beautiful spectacle which I saw. Soon the light quietly faded away and darkness came on the scene. With perfect quietness and peace of mind I came down to earth. Something said to me, "this is a specimen of the brightness, of 'His coming.'"

Affectionately, your father,

George N. Briggs

# Afterword

In *The Sense of the Past,* Henry James has the young historian Ralph Pendrel, the improbable author of "An Essay in the Aid of Reading History," reflect that "recovering the lost was at all events . . . much like entering the enemy's lines to get back one's dead for burial." That this novel remained unfinished at James's death should not surprise us. For it sets out the habitually insoluble quandary of the historian: how to live in two worlds at once; how to take the broken, mutilated remains of something or someone from the "enemy lines" of the documented past and restore it to life or give it a decent interment in our own time and place.

Pendrel yearns for the kind of communion with the dead denied him by the customary practises of his profession. "He wanted the unimaginable accidents, the little notes of truth for which the common lens of history, however the scowling muse might bury her nose, was not sufficiently fine. He wanted evidence of a sort for which there had never been documents enough or for which documents mainly, however multiplied, would never *be* enough." And he succeeds only through a metaphysical mystery by which, in the year 1910, he walks through the front door of the London house left to him in a legacy and enters 1820.

Without this convenient epiphany, historians are left forever chasing shadows, painfully aware of their inability ever to reconstruct a dead world in its completeness, however thorough or revealing their documentation. Of course, they make do with other work: the business of formulating problems, of supplying explanations about cause and effect. But the certainty of such answers always remains contingent on their unavoidable remoteness from their subjects. We are doomed to be forever hailing someone who has just gone around the corner and out of earshot.

Both the stories offered here play with the teasing gap separating a lived event and its subsequent narration. Although both follow the documented record with some closeness, they are works of the imagination, not scholarship. Both dissolve the certainties of events into the multiple possibilities of alternative narrations. Thus, General Wolfe dies many deaths, and though a verdict is rendered and a confession delivered in the case of John Webster, the ultimate truth about how George Parkman met his end remains obscure. Even resting places for last remains are cloudy with ambiguity. Wolfe's body, embalmed on the voyage home, is buried in a modest church, while an immense monument is part of the imperial pantheon at Westminster Abbey. The dismembered parts of George Parkman are given proper interment in the consecrated ground at Mount Auburn Cemetery whereas John Webster's intact corpse has to be left in an unmarked grave to escape either hostile vandals or the "resurrection men," one of whose histories had condemned him.

These are stories then, of broken bodies, uncertain ends, indeterminate consequences. And in keeping with the self-disrupting nature of the narratives, I have deliberately dislocated the conventions by which histories establish coherence and persuasiveness. Avoiding the framing of time-sequences supplied by historical chronologies, the stories begin with abrupt interventions—like windows suddenly opened—and end with many things unconcluded. (The "Conclusion" that every doctoral adviser urges on his students as a professional obligation has always seemed to my notoriously inconclusive temperament to be so much wishful thinking.) Both stories end with accounts at odds with each other as to what has happened, as to the significance of the deaths and the character of the protagonists. Only the genuinely innocent figure of the ex-Governor of Massachusetts, his signature on the execution warrant, rises in his spiritual dream world, levitating above the gory mess of historical reality.

Though these stories may at times appear to observe the discursive conventions of history, they are in fact historical novellas, since some passages (the soldier with Wolfe's army, for example) are pure inventions, based, however, on what documents suggest. This is not to say, I should emphasise, that I scorn the boundary between fact and fiction. It is merely to imply that even in the most austere scholarly report from the archives, the inventive faculty—selecting, pruning, editing, commenting, interpreting, delivering judgements—is in full play. This is not a naïvely relativist position that insists that the lived past is *nothing* more than an artificially designed text. (Despite the criticism of dug-in positivists, I know of no thoughtful commentator on historical narrative who seriously advances this view.) But it does accept the rather banal axiom that claims for historical knowledge must always be fatally circumscribed by the character and prejudices of its narrator.

"It was when life was framed in death that the picture was really hung up," observes James's historian arrived in England in search of the stopped pulse of time. And the two deaths reported in these stories both become public events, just as in their dramatically different ways the bodies become public possessions. In both cases, alternative accounts of the event compete for credibility, both for contemporaries and for posterity. There, however, all similarity ends, for in the case of General Wolfe, the competition is one of celebration: of the construction of a patriotic martyrology; of the invention of a myth that could affirm the peculiar destiny of the Anglo-American Empire. George Parkman's death, in extreme contrast, is a squalid and shocking reproach to the governing class of Harvard and Boston. In this second case, the competing versions of what had happened and why were not allowed to ornament each other over time and in different genres, as in the Wolfe history. Instead, they had to be rushed forward to satisfy the highly compressed interests of justice, punishment and oblivion. The striking sparseness of documentation in the Harvard University Archives (compared with equally extraordinary richness in the Massachusetts Historical Society records) suggests how complete the oblivion has been.

Both stories are, of course, Parkman stories, and although I arrived with happy inadvertence at the George Parkman calamity by pondering the career of his more famous nephew, there seem, in retrospect, to be compulsions and obsessions that run through the entire tragic dynasty. The Parkman inheritance—lying at the core of Boston's own ambiguous *historical* relationship with old England and New England—deeply colours both stories. In flight from the expectations of that inheritance— Unitarian, moneyed, reasonable, Harvardian—

Francis Parkman seeks the prairies and the forests (just as other writers of his generation, Dana and Melville, sought the open ocean). George Parkman journeys equally far, to the asylums of the insane in Paris, but fails to break free of the obligations of his property, and becomes instead its rigorous steward and, ultimately, its victim.

Family obligations lie heavily on all the protagonists and shape their histories. James Wolfe's career is devoted to satisfying the stern expectations of his father, but the hero dies without ever reconciling his implacable mother to an intended marriage. Benjamin West creates a family fortune from his inspired fabrication, while John Webster's disaster arises directly from his pathetic inability to meet his own and others' expectations of a Harvard College family. While Francis Parkman, Sr., bears the immediate brunt of the macabre tragedy, his historian son stands remote from the scene, lost in the forest darkness of Pontiac's Indian Conspiracy.

Family histories, then, do not presuppose family pieties. Mrs. Wolfe and Katherine Lowther share different and absolutely opposed memories of the General; the Widow Webster and her sister Amelia have equally irreconcilable memories of the Professor; the Reverend George Putnam and George Parkman, Jr., come close to legal proceedings against each other, merely to establish the true character of the murder victim.

All these things — memory, property, dynasty —

are braided throughout the stories and, though both travel the Atlantic this way and that (stopping on the Azores rocks from time to time), they are also both Boston histories, caught (as I sometimes am myself) between smoothly related consolatory pasts and chaotic, sometimes brutal disturbances of the present.

In its original Greek sense the word "historia" meant an inquiry, but historians ever since have differed on the implications of the term, sometimes imagining themselves lined up behind opposing platoons commanded by Herodotus or Thucydides. In the historian of the Peloponnesian War, modern historians have seen an early paragon of objectivity, of critical use of sources, of dispassionate analytical investigation. To others it is exactly the absence of these qualities which so recommends Herodotus: his relish for gossip, his intuitive understanding of the idiosyncrasies of climate and geography, his primitive ethnography, his unabashed subjectivities, the winning mishmash of hearsay and record, real and fantastic.

But to have an *inquiry,* whether into the construction of a legend, or the execution of a crime, is surely to require the telling of stories. And so the asking of questions and the relating of narratives need not, I think, be mutually exclusive forms of historical representation. And if in the end we must be satisfied with nothing more than broken lines of communication to the past; if denied Ralph

Pendrel's mystical transport across the centuries, we stumble only on "unimaginable accidents," and our flickering glimpses of dead worlds fall far short of ghostly immersion, that perhaps is still enough to be going on with.

# A Note on Sources

This book is a work of the imagination that chronicles historical events. In both parts, the narratives are based on primary sources. In many cases, including some of the most unlikely episodes—George Parkman's epiphany with the human dermis for example—I have faithfully followed accounts given in letters and journals. Testimony and arguments presented at the trial of John Webster are quoted verbatim from the record.

Two kinds of passages are purely imagined fiction. In the first kind (as in the soldier's witness of the Battle of Quebec) the narrative has been constructed from a number of contemporary documents. The more purely fictitious dialogues (such as Marshal Tukey's conversation with Ephraim Littlefield) are worked up from my own understanding of the sources as to how such a scene might have taken place.

## A Note on Sources

There is a small but suggestive dossier of letters in Wolfe's hand preserved at the Houghton Library, Harvard University, as well as a more substantial collection of "Wolfiana" dealing with his memorialisation.

Published sources on his life include Beckles Willson, *The Life and Letters of James Wolfe* (London, 1909). A. G. Doughty and G. W. Parmelee, *The Siege of Quebec,* 6 vols. (Quebec, 1901), has exhaustive documentation. Volumes IV–VI contain, *inter alia,* the journals of Major Moncrief of the Royal Engineers; John Johnson, Clerk and Quartermaster-Sergeant of the Fifty-Eighth Regiment of Foot; the "Genuine Letters from a Volunteer in the British Service at Quebec" material from the Townshend papers; as well as superb photographs of weapons, uniform and buildings. Doughty and Parmelee claim that the bullet that killed Wolfe ended up in the possession of King Edward VII, part of a collection of "death messengers" said to have changed the whole aspect of history and which included the fatal projectiles that caused the death of Lord Nelson, General Burgoyne and others. Their anthology also makes abundantly clear the discrepancies between the many accounts of Wolfe's final moments (III: 223–5). West's painting is categorically dismissed as "absolutely valueless as a historic representation."

Among the candidates for memorialisation as supporters of the dying general were, according to different reports, an artillery man called James who had served at Louisbourg and Quebec and a Highland officer called Macdougall. John Knox, in his *Historical Journal of the Campaign in North America for the years 1757, 1758, 1759 and 1760* (London, 1769), gives two further names of the four men said to have attended Wolfe: James Henderson, a volunteer of the Twenty-Eighth Regiment, and Lieutenant Henry Brown of Louisbourg Grenadiers and Twenty-Second Regiment. Many reports refer to another unnamed junior officer, and I have taken advantage of these uncertainties to use first-hand accounts of the action in the construction of my own witness.

Other important primary sources may be found in H. R. Casgrain [Francis Parkman's archival collaborator], *La Guerre du Canada,* 2 vols. (Quebec, 1891), and in *The Northcliffe Collection* (Ottawa, 1926).

Many accounts of the battle for Quebec were published at its bicentennial. Among the better accounts are Christopher Hibbert, *Wolfe at Quebec* (London, 1959); Brian Connell, *The Plains of Abraham* (London, 1959); Robin Reilly, *The Rest Is Fortune* (London, 1960); and C. P. Stacey, *Quebec, 1759* (New York, 1959).

# A Note on Sources

On physiognomies and likenesses, see J. Clarence Webster, *A Study of the Portraiture of James Wolfe* (1925). See also idem *Wolfiana* (nd).

## BENJAMIN WEST

James Galt, *The Life of Benjamin West* (London, 1820), is now thought apocryphal to a large extent and self-serving, and is generally discredited as dependable biography. But it still has great value as a source for inspired, mythic self-promotion.

More recent studies include: Grose Evans, *Benjamin West and the Taste of His Times* (Carbondale, Illinois, 1959); Helmut von Erffa and Allen Staley, *The Paintings of Benjamin West* (New Haven, 1986); Anne Uhry Abrams, *The Valiant Hero: Benjamin West and Grand-Style History Painting* (Washington, D.C., 1985).

*Benjamin West: American Painter at the English Court* (Baltimore, 1989) is a first-rate exhibition catalogue and has a helpful scholarly bibliography.

## PARKMAN

Massachusetts Historical Society, *Proceedings,* second series (1892, 1894); O. B. Frothingham, Proceedings of the Massachusetts Historical Society (1894); Charles H. Farnham, *Life of Francis Parkman* (1900); Mason Wade, *Francis Parkman, Heroic Historian* (New York, 1942); (ed) *The Jour-*

*nals of Francis Parkman,* 2 vols. (Boston, 1947); Howard Doughty, *Francis Parkman* (New York, 1962); David Levin, *History as Romantic Art: Bancroft, Motley, Parkman* (1959); *France and England in North America* (New York, 1983).

## DEATH OF A HARVARD MAN

My account of the murder of George Parkman is drawn both from testimony given at the trial and from the rich supplementary documentation concerning all the principals (including the prosecution and defence attorneys) preserved in the Massachusetts Historical Society. Many of these documents are presented verbatim (though sometimes abridged) in the text with misspelling and broken syntax unaltered. The clemency petitions to Governor Briggs, Briggs's own letters to his daughter, Amelia Nye Hickling's letters to her sister in the Azores, George Bemis's journal entries, John Webster's letters from jail and George Parkman's letters from Europe are all such documentary sources.

Other primary sources consulted for Boston's and Harvard's reaction to the murder and the trial include the papers of Nahum Capen, John Clifford, Frederick Cunningham, Frederick Lewis Gay, Edward Everett, Oliver Wendell Holmes, Horace Mann, Francis Parkman, Sr., George Parkman, William Prescott, Lemuel Shaw and John White Webster.

I also made use of the Harvard University Archive collection of newspaper clippings, printed legal opinions from Massachusetts and other states and sermons.

SECONDARY SOURCES

There are two modern books on the Webster trial: Robert Sullivan, *The Disappearance of Dr. Parkman* (Boston, 1971) (emphasis on the legal history); Helen Thomson, *Murder at Harvard* (Boston, 1971).

For mid-nineteenth-century Boston and problems of police: Oscar Handlin, *Boston's Immigrants* (Cambridge, Mass., 1979); Roger Lane, *Policing the City, Boston, 1822–1885* (Cambridge, Mass., 1967); Edward H. Savage, *A Chronological History of the Boston Watch and Police from 1631 to 1865 or Boston by Daylight and Gaslight* (Boston, 1865).

For contemporary perceptions of the Boston patriciate, "Our First Men" A Calendar of Wealth, Fashion and Gentility (Boston, 1846).

For the flavor and social climate of the time, the best sources are contemporary newspapers like the Boston *Evening Transcript* or *Gleason's Pictorial Companion,* from which the portrait of Marshal Tukey was taken.

# A Note on Sources

For biographic (and invariably eulogising) biographies of some of the principals see Frederic Hathaway Chase, *Lemuel Shaw, Chief Justice* (Boston, 1918); William C. Richards, *Great in Goodness, A Memoir of George N. Briggs* (Boston, 1866); Francis George Shaw, *Robert Gould Shaw 1776–1853* (Boston, 1941); Oliver Wendell Holmes, *George Parkman, A Lecture to the Medical College, November 7th, 1850;* Samuel Eliot Morison, *Three Centuries of Harvard* (Cambridge, Mass., 1936).

On the trial, the official version is George Bemis, *Report of the Case of John W. Webster, Erving Professor of Chemistry and Mineralogy in Harvard University* (Boston, 1850). Newspaper reports of the trial differ, sometimes quite radically, even when they claim "stenographic" or even "phonographic" transcription. The version, for example, rushed into print in the summer of 1850 by James Stone was much disapproved of by Bemis and Clifford as in serious error. But many of the reports are nonetheless invaluable for giving, in fine print, an unmistakable impression of the atmosphere of the proceedings and the demeanour of witnesses, lawyers, the bench and the accused.

On the nineteenth-century Azores, C. Alice Baker, *A Summer in the Azores* (Boston, 1882); Captain Boid, *A Description of the Azores or Western Islands from Personal Observation* (London, 1834).

## PHOTOGRAPHIC
### ACKNOWLEDGEMENTS

*page 2*   McCord Museum of Canadian History, Montreal
*between pages 18 and 19*   National Gallery of Canada,
Ottawa

*page 29*   Ashmolean Museum, Oxford, England
*page 35*   Top: Kimbell Art Museum, Fort Worth, Texas.
Bottom: The Board of Trustees of the National Museums &
Galleries on Merseyside [Walker Art Gallery, Liverpool]
*page 38   Self-Portrait;* Benjamin WEST; National Gallery
of Art, Washington; Andrew W. Mellon Collection
*pages 62, 72, 90, 92, 109, 113, 117, 127, 128, 134, 140, 211, 217,
221, 275*   Massachusetts Historical Society

Simon Schama was born in London, in 1945, and studied history at Cambridge University, where from 1966 to 1976 he was a Fellow of Christ's College. He is now Mellon Professor in the Social Sciences and Senior Associate at the Center for European Studies at Harvard University. He is the author of *Patriots and Liberators: Revolution in the Netherlands (1780–1813)* (1977); *Two Rothschilds and the Land of Israel* (1979); and *The Embarrassment of Riches: An Interpretation of Dutch Culture in the Golden Age* (1987). His most recent book, *Citizens: A Chronicle of the French Revolution* (1989), was *The Yorkshire Post* Book of the Year and won the N.C.R. 1990 Book Award for nonfiction. He lives with his wife and two children in Massachusetts.

A NOTE ON THE TYPE

This book was set in a digitized version of Caledonia, a face
designed by W. A. Dwiggins (1880–1956). It belongs to the
family of printing types called "modern face" by printers—
a term used to mark the change in style of type letters that
occurred about 1800. Caledonia borders on the general
design of Scotch Roman, but is more freely
drawn than that letter.

Composed by The Sarabande Press,
New York, New York
Printed and bound by
Fairfield Graphics, Fairfield, Pennsylvania
Designed by Iris Weinstein